HAUNTED HIKES

of NEW HAMPSHIRE

Marianne O'Connor

PublishingWorks, Inc.
Exeter, NH
2008

2nd printing, 2008

Maps © 2008 by Tim Trotter.
Illustrations © 2008 by Marcia LeMay.
Photos by the author unless otherwise noted.

PublishingWorks, Inc.,
60 Winter Street
Exeter, NH 03833
603-778-9883
For Sales and Orders:
1-800-738-6603 or 603-772-7200

Designed by: Kat Mack & Anna Godard
Cover design by Kat Mack. Glow in the dark cover printing by Phoenix Color.

LCCN: 2007937401
ISBN: 1-933002-59-X
ISBN-13: 978-1-933002-59-0

For Leah and Lynn

Contents

FOREWORD

Haunted Hikes of New Hampshire celebrates unique and obscure stories behind many special and less well-known places you can visit.

Each walk, hike and exploration adds your own story to the landscape. You always remember a walk or hike not only by the weather and what you saw, but by who accompanied you. The echoes of laughter and falling leaves will help you to create your own personal "storied" landscape of memories that can last a lifetime—if you make the modest effort to get outside and explore these special places!

The Forest Society is particularly proud of a statewide legacy of intentional land conservation. We've protected many special places (and a treasure trove of stories the landscape contains) for future generations. We support connecting residents with a strong sense of place that, with time, will become the basis of a land ethic that grows with every hiking experience. Learning about local history, legends and lore—even the creepy, odd, scary or bizarre stories you may never have heard before—is a vital aspect of forest preservation.

Three of the Forest Society's own special permanent Forest Reservations are included among the Haunted Hikes: Madame Sherri Forest in Chesterfield, Indian Arrowhead Forest in Surry, and Monson Village in Milford and Hollis. These sites are open to the public and offer easy walks or short hikes to scenic and historic resources. They are open air museums, where artifacts and history are preserved in place, protected in our privately owned forest reservations. Please respect the land and its stories, honor the ghosts of our predecessors and they, in turn, will welcome your visit.

I hope that Marianne O'Connor's book will spark your interest in New Hampshire history by providing natural places for families to explore and learn. Now get out there and enjoy the Haunted Hikes of New Hampshire!

David Anderson, Director of Education
Society for the Protection of New Hampshire Forests

Hike Safe!
Have Fun! But Be Safe!
Know the Hiker Responsibility Code
You are responsible for yourself so be prepared:

1. **With knowledge and gear**. Become self reliant by learning about the terrain, conditions, local weather and your equipment before you start.

2. **To leave your plans**. Tell someone where you are going, the trails you are hiking, when you will return and your emergency plans.

3. **To stay together**. When you start as a group, hike as a group, end as a group. Pace your hike to the slowest person.

4. **To turn back**. Weather changes quickly in the mountains. Fatigue and unexpected conditions can also affect your hike. Know your limitations and when to postpone your hike. The mountains will be there another day.

5. **For emergencies**. Even if you are headed out for just an hour, an injury, severe weather or a wrong turn could become life threatening. Don't assume you will be rescued; know how to rescue yourself.

6. **To share the hiker code with others**.

For more info visit www.hikesafe.com

The Hiker Responsibility Code was developed and is endorsed by New Hampshire Fish and Game and White Mountain National Forest

Reprinted with permission from Hikesafe.

Legend for hike difficulty:

One ghost:	Easy, child friendly
Two ghosts:	Moderate
Three ghosts:	Difficult, best for experienced hikers
Four ghosts:	Challenging, not recommended for children or inexperienced dogs

MAP LEGEND

🏠	Gould House (Monson)
●	Named Location
■	Foundations
⚏	Cemetery
▲	AMC Huts
P	Parking Area
★	Point of Interest
✝	Gravesite
▲	Peak
············	Hiking Trails
○○○○○○	Bike Path/Greenway
——	Local Roads
⊣123⊢	NH State Highways
⟨302⟩	U.S. Hwy
⟨93⟩	Interstate/State Highway
▬▬▬	River/Stream
——	25m Elevation Contours 10m Elevation Contours on Madame Sherri, Monson, and Mt Caesar
┼┼┼┼┼	Railroad Tracks
-----	Town Line
▱	Conservation Area
▬	Lake/Pond
Temple	Town Name

Monson Village
Milford-Hollis, NH

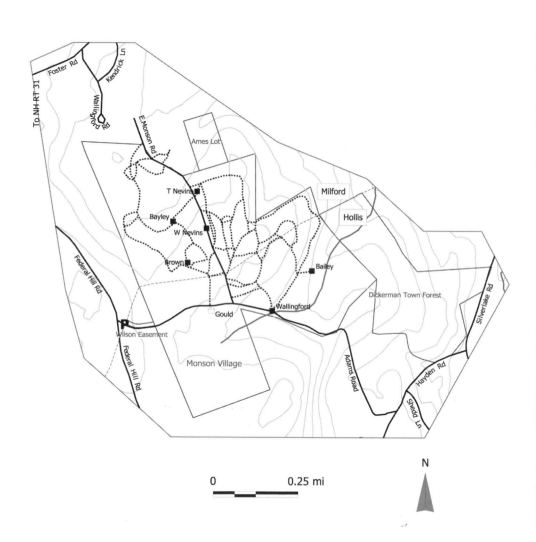

1 The Ghost Towns of Monson Center and Indian Arrowhead Forest

Monson Village, Milford

A walk through Monson Village, the first inland pioneer settlement of New Hampshire, is a stroll through a ghost town. Pass through the entrance gate, and follow the main trail to the small blue Gould House, and it is clear to see why this place has become a favorite for history buffs and ghost hunters alike. In fact, many residents feel so strongly about the area, they fought to protect it from development. In 1998 the land was eyed by developers planning a major subdivision off Federal Hill Road. Neighbors who owned the property adjacent to the proposed development donated over one hundred acres of their own land to the Society for the Protection of New Hampshire's Forests to stop the bulldozers. The strategy worked, and today, Monson Village is owned by the Forest Society.

Monson Village has come under investigation by Ghost Quest, a paranormal research group in New England. Researchers video taped and recorded strange sounds and unique phenomena which can be seen on their website. Other unusual sightings have been reported; some have heard drums beating and seen flashes of lights through the woods. Perhaps it is the cry of lost souls searching for their final resting spot, long ago forgotten and lying in ruins under the earth.

Though the village is located in the town of Milford, along the Hollis town line, the area was once a part of Massachusetts. In the 1600s the Massachusetts Bay Colony awarded land tracts to distinguished citizens: war heroes, successful businessmen, etc. These fortunate citizens organized townships in what are now Nashua, Brookline, Amherst, and Hollis. In 1673 the township of Dunstable was chartered,

Monson Village has come under investigation by Ghost Quest, a paranormal research group in New England.

which included these areas and others along the Souhegan River. In 1741 a new state line was drawn and Dunstable broke off into smaller sections, leaving Monson Village in the state of New Hampshire. Monson was first incorporated in 1746 after the first settlers moved up from Massachusetts. Eventually, the residents of Monson gave up their charter following years of struggle and debate about how to tax themselves for building a town meetinghouse and where it should be located. A restored colonial era house belonging to the town clock maker, Joseph Gould, stands as Monson's headquarters. Gould also served the town as a selectman, constable, and pound keeper. The house is now a small museum. Monson's most famous "daughter" was Anna (Kendrick) Pierce, mother of U.S. President Franklin Pierce.

The remaining citizens of Monson voted in 1770 to divide the town land. A petition to the state authorities stated:

"The land in the centre of Monson is so very poor, broken and barren—it cannot admit many settlers. We have no prospect of ever building a meeting house, anyways, to accommodate us, by which difficulties we think the gospel will not be settled among us while in the present situation. We therefore pray." (From George Ramsdell's *History of Milford*.)

THE HIKE

What is left of Monson Village today is a 215-acre tract of open fields and woodlands. Ancient cellar holes are all that remain of the salt-box Cape houses and log cabins that were once home to the villagers. Each of the cellar holes can be traced to the families who settled here, with historic markers that describe the fate of each family. Maps are available at the Gould House to lead you down the various paths to the homesteads. Each path is marked by hand-carved wooden signs. The main paths through Monson Center are wide gravel roads, with easy wooded side trails that lead to the cellar holes. Take a self-guided tour, and enjoy the stroll along Adams Road lined with blue bird boxes. A walk down East Monson Road will take you to a side path leading to the site of Dr. Brown's home, the village doctor from 1746 to 1770.

From the gate at Adams Road to Gould House and the loop of East Monson Road to West Monson Road is approximately 2.5 miles.

Time:	Allow 1–2 hours
Parking:	Free
Open:	Dusk till dawn
Things to look for:	Bluebird activity, wildlife viewing and ancient cellar holes. Gould House open on intermittent basis. Free Admission.
For more info:	www.spnhf.org
Managed and owned by:	Society for the Protection of New Hampshire Forests

WHERE IS THIS PLACE?

Take the NH Rte. 101 bypass to Rte. 13 east toward Hollis/ Brookline at the end of the ramp. Next take Emerson Road, the second left off Rte. 13. The first right is Federal Hill Road, which follows for 2.4 miles to a gated gravel road and a gate on the left hand side. Do not park at the gate, but along the side of the entrance road. Open dawn to dusk. Maps are available at the Gould House.

Thomas Gould House, restored Monson Village.

Indian Arrowhead Forest Preserve

The southwestern quadrant of Surry lies between Westmoreland and Keene. In this corner, just off Rte. 12, is a hidden gem of local history. Surry was incorporated in 1769, and the first settler was a man feared by even the most savage of Indians. Peter Hayward, along with his fierce and intimidating dog, was an enemy of the Indians. The Indians were afraid to kill him, fearing that his ferocious dog would avenge his death. Hayward served as a protector for other new families in the Westmoreland area. After conquering raiding Indians, he then served in the Revolutionary War, at the battle of Bunker Hill, wearing a leather apron. At his side during the battle was his loyal and dangerous pooch. When Hayward settled in Surry, over two hundred other early settlers followed him. They saw in him a hero and protector.

The hills and valleys surrounding Surry are picturesque, but it was what lay beneath the hills that attracted the settlers. Gold and silver deposits were discovered in the 1780s, and many descended upon the land to search for riches found in the mineral deposits. This led to the opening of silver and gold mines on Mine Ledge, near Indian Arrowhead reserve. Geologically, this area is known for carrying deposits of copper, gold, and silver that can be found in trace quantities in quartz still today. By the 1800s the unprofitable silver mine shut down completely, but many of the miners stayed. The last miner was a war veteran named William Ritter who never left the run-down camp. He died there in 1827, alone, his remains later discovered by authorities. Visitors claim to still hear the faint tapping of his pick as he searches for that ore of silver that will make him rich beyond his wildest dreams.

On the top of Arrowhead look for a petroglyph of an Indian bow and arrow chiseled into granite. For many years, this unique carving was believed to be left by the Indians. The arrow points southeast to Keene and Mt. Monadnock. Similar bow and arrow carvings appeared throughout southwestern Surry. Eventually, the strange rock carvings were attributed to a local man, and a descendent of some early settlers, William Mason (1832–1912). He was described as peculiar and strange; he was most likely autistic, with a clever and creative flare for the primitive Indian craftsmanship. Mason never married and lived quietly on his brother's farm, reading and wandering the mountains and hills with his axe. He lived to be eighty years old and died of a heart attack in 1912 as he attempted to roll a giant boulder into a brook.

THE HIKE

Arrowhead Forest is located in Surry, a short five-mile drive from Keene. The property is owned by The Society for the Protection of New Hampshire Forests.

You can hike to the top of Arrowhead Mountain and search for the bow and arrow on the giant rock. The trail through the forest leads you through the woods with abandoned wells, foundations, and cellar holes. There are hidden graves here, stone walls, and wagon wheels. They are the scattered remnants from the early settlers. You can also look for minerals like quartz with deposits of silver, copper, and galena, a lead ore mineral. Many of the miners could have believed that a fortune awaited them from the earth, but it was not to be. If you find a treasure, be sure to hide it away or old Will Ritter will rise from his grave in search of your find!

The forest reservation is managed under the Society for the Protection of New Hampshire Forests.

CRAIN ROAD HIKE

One other area of interest in Surry is an equally eerie hike through a ghost town along old Rte. 12A off Crain Road. This area is reached via Rte. 12A to Crain Road on the right. At the end of the old village you will see a gate and gravel road. Park at the meetinghouse next to the graveyard. A walk through the graveyard offers the delightful discovery that some Crain family members are buried here, including, one named Ichabod! The old road begins at a gated entrance. Land here is protected by Army Corps of Engineers. There are a total of seven cellar holes and ruins among the apple orchards. It is an easy one mile walk which brings you to a junction of Rte. 12A.

Indian Arrowhead Forest

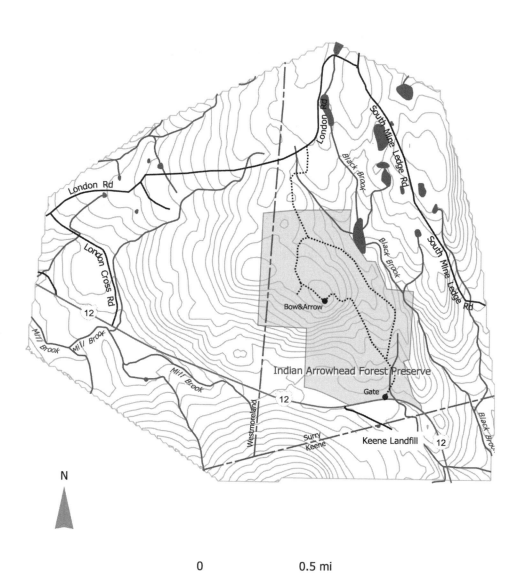

WHERE IS THIS PLACE?

The Arrowhead Forest Preserve is located in the town of Surry. It can be reached by following NH Rte. 101 to the junction of Rte. 12 north. A secret access trail is located on the right side of Rte.12 approximately 5.6 miles from the Rte. 101 junction. You can park at the gate, but the area is very overgrown. Trails along the reservation are well marked. The hike to the arrow head rock is an easy 2 mile loop start to finish from the gate. At .3 miles from the gate, the trail meets at a junction with a sign. For an easier climb, turn right. For a more difficult hike, turn left. The old arrow head etching is over 100 years old and fairly faded. This 293-acre forest is owned by The Society for the Protection of New Hampshire Forests.

From parking area on Rte. 12 to Arrow Head Rock ascending difficult route and descending easy route, approximately 2 miles.

Time:	Allow 1–2 hours for exploration
Parking :	Free
Open:	Dusk till dawn
Things to look for:	Cellar holes; remnants of early farmers and settlers; rocks and minerals containing traces of copper, silver and hematite; Ghosts.
Managed and owned by:	Society for the Protection of New Hampshire Forests
For more info:	www.spnhf.org
For info on NH's rocks and minerals:	www.gsnhonline.org

Madame Sherri Forest
West Chesterfield, NH

Hiking Trails
Indian Pond - 45 min roundtrip
Ann Stokes Loop - 2 miles
Daniels Loop - 1.8 miles

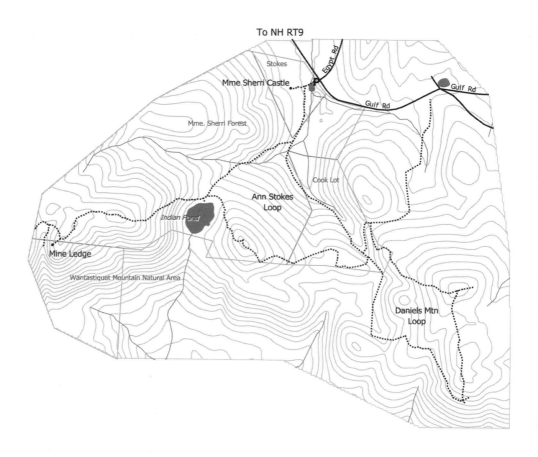

To NH RT9

Stokes

Egypt Rd

Mme Sherri Castle

Gulf Rd

Mme. Sherri Forest

Gulf Rd

Cook Lot

Ann Stokes
Loop

Indian Pond

Mine Ledge

Wantastiquet Mountain Natural Area

Daniels Mtn
Loop

N

0   0.25 mi

2 Madame Sherri: A Haunted Castle Hike in West Chesterfield

Ahike through the eerie castle ruins at the Madame Sherri's Forest in West Chesterfield will send tingles up your spine. This 488-acre forest preserve has hikes for all levels of ability. The forest land around the chateau was donated for conservation to the Society for Protection of New Hampshire Forests by Ann Stokes.

Antoinette De Lilas sang in the Cabaret in Paris before coming to New York in 1911 with her much younger husband, Andre Riela, a silent film actor. The couple changed their name to Sherri and started a costume design business that was extremely successful. Sherri designed many of the theatrical costumes for New York theatre shows including the Ziegfield Follies. She was a savvy business woman and her creativity and flare put her in high demand. Andre died unexpectedly in 1924. By then, Madame Sherri had become rich, and enjoyed a flamboyant lifestyle of elegant parties and high fashion. She often spent summer vacations with friends in the Chesterfield area and loved the quiet country charm it offered. Spofford Lake was an artistic retreat for many involved in the theatre, and Madame Sherri was so attracted to the area she bought farm land on Gulf Road and on the back side of Mt. Wantastiquet and commissioned the building of an elaborate fifteen-room "castle" where she would spend her summers hosting wild parties. Those who remember her say she drove around Chesterfield in a Packard driven by her chauffeur. She was known to wear a fur coat with absolutely nothing on

Madame Sherri, courtesy of Brattleboro Historical Society.

Some say that touching the stair case will elicit faint sounds of ghostly waltz music.

underneath. This, no doubt, created a whirlwind of gossip, and rumor had it that the chateau was a brothel.

Over time, the Madame's health and mental functioning deteriorated and she was forced to abandon the castle. Her remaining years were spent as a ward of the state in a Brattleboro, Vermont, nursing home. She was indigent and in poor mental and physical health, a mere shell of the beauty she had been. The castle had fallen into ruin over years of neglect and was looted and vandalized. In 1962 it was gutted by fire, most likely set by arsonists. Her fortune gone, Madame Sherri died three years later, poor and alone, and was finally buried in a Brattleboro cemetery with a simple stone. Strangely, the sale of Madame Sherri's property and "farm house" occurred on the day of her death. All that remains of Sherri's castle home is a stone foundation, fireplace, and winding granite staircase the locals have named, "Stairway to Heaven."

The site is said to be haunted. Some say that touching the staircase will elicit faint sounds of ghostly waltz music. There are reports that a shimmering specter of Madame Sherri can be seen gliding down the stone staircase, eager to greet her guests from the shadows of yesterday.

"Stairway to Heaven" stone staircase of the chateau.

In 1991, Anne Stokes, who owned the Madame Sherri castle property, donated this portion of land to the Society for the Protection of New Hampshire Forests for Conservation.

THE HIKES

After parking at the main parking terminus on Gulf Road, a kiosk displays photos and information on the former chateaux and the life and times of Madame Sherri. The ruins of the castle are only twenty yards off to the right hand side and up a short drive where you'll see the impressive staircase. Climbing the stairs is a dizzying pursuit, but one that will open your eyes to the rare and magnificent character the castle emanated in its glory days. After visiting the castle ruins, there are a number of different trails to take either around Indian Pond, or out to Mine Ledge on Mt. Wantastiquet or Daniels Mountain. Each hike offers sweeping views of the region. The Ann Stokes loop and Daniel's Mountain Loop are considered moderate hikes and can be accessed directly from the main parking area.

ANN STOKES LOOP:

After exploring the castle, return to the main trail and follow signs to the trail passing a pond and turning left toward Daniels Mt. (1,225'), where there are some nice views from the ledges looking out over Chesterfield. This loop is two miles long.

DANIELS MOUNTAIN LOOP:

A 1.8 mile loop over moderate terrain with some steep sections to the summit of Daniels Mt. and has two more views.

MINE LEDGE—MT. WANTASTIQUET (1,335'):

Bearing right at the map mailbox, this trail will take you out toward Mt. Wantastiquet and Mine Ledge. Legend goes that the Native Indians used these ledges as a lookout to spy on the activities at Fort Dummer. The cliffs on Mt. Wantastiquet offer great views to Brattleboro and Mine Ledge has the best view of all. The trails here are not as obvious as the other trails in the forest, so it's important to watch where you're going, especially with the thick carpet of fallen leaves on the trail.

Ann Stokes Loop:	A moderate 2 mile hike through hemlocks and rugged slopes.
Time :	Allow 1.5 hours
Parking:	Free
What to look for:	From the main terminus at Gulf Road look for Madame Sherri's castle ruins.
Daniels Mountain Loop:	A moderate 1.8 mile hike, some steep sections. Trail is accessible via the main parking area and east leg of Ann Stokes Loop.
Time:	1.5–2 hours
Parking:	Free
What to look for:	amazing views and wildlife.
For more info:	www.spnhf.org
Managed and owned by:	Society for the Protection of New Hampshire Forests
For more info:	www.chesterfieldoutdoors.com

WHERE IS THIS PLACE?

The Madame Sherri Forest is located in West Chesterfield, New Hampshire, about ten miles from Keene near the Vermont State border. Follow Rte. 9 West toward Brattleboro, VT. Just before crossing the Connecticut River into VT, turn left onto Mountain Road (next to a motel). Go 0.1 miles, then bear left at the fork onto Gulf Road. Continue for about 2.2 miles to the property entrance.

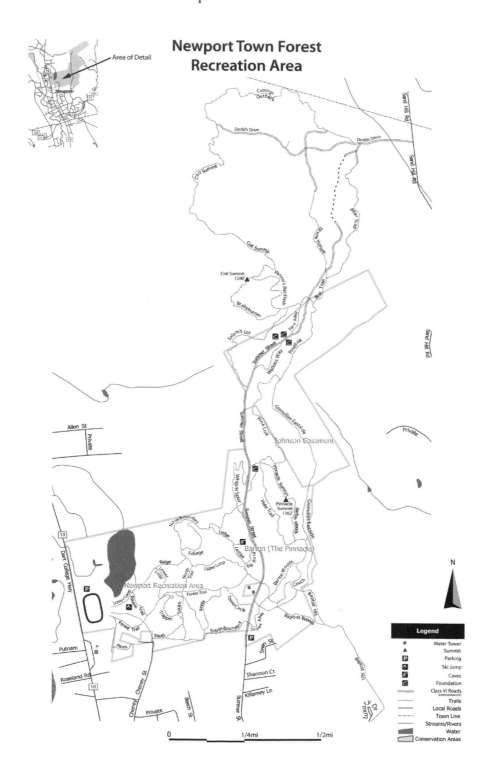

Newport Town Forest
Recreation Area

3 Black History on the Mountains

The story of a small group of freed African Americans and their journey to New Hampshire began with a man named Vance (Richard) Coit from Connecticut. At the turn of the nineteenth century, a community of blacks lived on the slopes of a mountain near the center of Newport and the neighboring town of Croydon. By the early 1800s most of the families had moved on. One of the most compelling stories from this period involves Vance Coit and the "connubial alliance" he shared with his white wife. The biracial couple was publicly scorned by most in the community at the time. Settlers who owned land near Coit Mt. were especially offended.

In the thick of a bleak night, some of the townsfolk discovered valuable equipment missing from their barns. The missing items were discovered on Coit's mountain top property by a band of locals eager to see the Negro man punished. Coit received a sentence of thirty-nine lashings in the public whipping post. By his side was his wife who begged officials to beat her instead. As Coit was whipped and blood gushed from his open sores, the woman soothed the wounds with a sponge soaked in rum. After the punishment had been fulfilled she drank the bloodied potation and earned public disdain for the rest of her life. But a burning question of justice remained like deep scars endured at the whipping post. Had Coit stolen the tools or were these items planted on his property in an attempt to buttress public contempt? Or was it just a slanderous story perpetuated to diminish his stature in history?

The town of Newport has expanded the Newport Town Forest to include a trail network that leads to the summit of Coit Mt. The town worked closely with the New Hampshire Historical Society in developing new trail names that fit with black history. These new trail names include Vance's Backlash and Brake Burner. There is even Salem's Lot, named for Salem Colby. These trails can be accessed through the town forest entry points near the Newport High School playing fields and on Summer Street. An intricate system of bike and foot trails lead through the forest and up and over Pinnacle Mt. which has outstanding views of the valley. The town is active in promoting bike races and racing teams that use these trails. The town has revised a path that leads to Coit's summit. It begins from a point on Old Summer St. in Newport, passes the trail to the Pinnacle and heads off to the left. The trails are popular among mountain bikers, and will soon be a more reliable trail system as new signs and blazes are placed by the town.

Bike riders report that someone is following or pursuing them through the woods.

There are ongoing and long-running reports of something living in the woods spooking the bikers. Most cyclists report that something or *someone* has chased them down the beaten paths. Most of the reports seem to happen during the night time hours. Park and Recreation Coordinator P.J. Lovely says he's heard the stories for years. Bike riders report that someone is following or pursuing them through the woods. I had a similar experience one day on Coit Mt. Though I did not feel "chased," I had the presence that someone else was with me on the mountain. I was eager to meet them and found myself pursuing them! Out of the corner of my eyes I caught a glimpse of a shadowy figure running through the trails. I never caught up or made contact, though the figure seemed only a short reach away. Perhaps the soul of Vance Coit pursues a justice that was denied. Or maybe a shadow in history is searching for something greater.

Other families of black descent moved to Coit Mt. from throughout New Hampshire. One was an emancipated slave named Salem Colby from Concord. There was Tom Billings and Robert Nott who were also involved in biracial unions, raising many eyebrows in town. Though some vilified their black skinned neighbors, others were on hand to upbraid local attitude and judgments.

As the town of Croydon celebrated its centennial celebration, dignitary Dr. Baron Stowe reminisced about a black resident named Scippio Page. The local white settlers used Page as a reference of bad moral character and told their children that Scip would be after the bad children who disobeyed their mothers. The good doctor admonished the townspeople and reminded them that Old Scip was indeed an honest man who minded his own business about town. Scip was a baker, and was active in the civic life of the Croydon community in which he lived and fought for acceptance.

Another famous black resident was Charles "Black Charlie" Hall who had been smuggled as a slave from Florida by a relative of the Deacon John Cutting in Newport. He lived openly and proudly as an escaped slave and married another African woman born in New Hampshire, named Ursula. They had nine children who all attended school in town. It appears that Charlie's residence and acceptance into the community life was made possible by movement through the Underground Railroad. Black Charlie was a popular community figure and was even photographed and had a poem written about him.

Many of these early free black settlers moved on to other parts of the region. Robert Nott went to Canada with his young white wife. Some left to relocate in New York and Vermont.

THE HIKE

Begin at the Newport Town forest where you can pick up the Forest Trail right behind the playing fields of Newport High. The Forest Trail intersects with other trails in the network. At about .25 miles it intersects with North Trail. Go left at the junction and

A chimney in a cellar hole off Summer Street near Coit Mt., Newport.

follow North Trail, then merge with the Upper Loop, which leads to Summer St, a double-wide track and the main artery of this system. Go north on Summer St. (left) and continue for .5 miles where The Pinnacle Summit Trail enters. The summit of Pinnacle offers gorgeous views and is only .3 miles short, but a steep hike to the top (elevation 1,362').

HIKE TO COIT MT.

From the junction of the Pinnacle Summit Trail continue north on Summer St. to Salem's Lot Trail. Salem's Lot enters on the left at .25 miles. Follow Salem's Lot for .3 miles to Vance's Backlash. Both Backlash and Brake Burner lead to the summit of Coit Mt. (elevation 1,590').

WHERE IS THIS PLACE?

The Newport Town Forest is located in the wooded forest behind Newport High School and various other access points. Take Interstate 89 north to Exit 9. Follow Rte. 103 west into Newport. Make a right onto Rte. 10 North. The High School and Recreation Complex will be on your right less than a mile from the center of town. Alternately, take Interstate 89 north to Exit 12. Make a left onto Rte. 11 and follow that west into Newport. Make a right onto Rte. 10 north. The High School and Recreation Complex will be on your right less than a mile from the center of town.

Mt. Caesar

In New Hampshire we name our mountains after figures of historic greatness: presidents, Indian chiefs, and brave frontiersmen who chartered vast unknown territories. Their names inspire majestic images of rocky cliffs and summits above the clouds. There are only a few mountains in North America named after slaves, two of which are in New Hampshire: Coit Mountain and Mt. Caesar, both named for African Americans who lived in these remote landscapes after their freedom from slavery.

In beautiful Swanzey, you will find four covered bridges and a picturesque New England Village community rich in history. The township was first settled in 1737 as Lower Ashulot, but the first settlers, all from Massachusetts, discovered that the boundaries of the township lay not under the jurisdiction of Massachusetts, but under that of New Hampshire. It was a great blow. Without the security of the militia provided by the Massachusetts Commonwealth, the settlers were subject to fierce Indian raids that left them terrorized. Several people were killed or captured as prisoners during the French and Indian War. Eventually, the settlers abandoned the tiny town and all of their buildings wcrc dcstroycd by fire.

Something had happened in the mountains, but neither of them could recall.

In 1753, much of the danger of Indian raids had passed and the township was once more re-granted under the name Swanzey in a new charter. The new settlers held optimistic views that a period of peace and prosperity would emerge. Many came from parts of Massachusetts that were considered liberal minded and strongly in favor of the Revolutionary War against Britain. The settlers agreed to pay a large sum of money and chose the Reverend Ezra Carpenter of Hull, Massachusetts, to be their new minister. He was a Harvard College graduate of 1720 and likely shared the progressive beliefs of pre-abolitionists that had begun to take hold. The minister and his family, including a wife and eight children, arrived in Swanzey in October of 1753 where he was given land by the townspeople.

Joining the Carpenter brood was a freed slave, possibly Caesar, known as "Freeman Caesar" to the locals. According to historic records, Freeman Caeser was the first Negro man in the region. Little is known about who Caesar was. He was likely a runaway slave from the Boston area who sought and found emancipation. Town legend has it that somewhere beyond the boundaries of the Mt. Caesar cemetery, Caesar himself is buried. But no one knows for sure the location of his grave. There is no historic explanation as to why the mountain was named after him, only that he lived there, and over time it became known as Caesar's mountain, or Mt. Caesar (962'). Much of the early records were destroyed.

Mt Caesar - Swanzey, NH

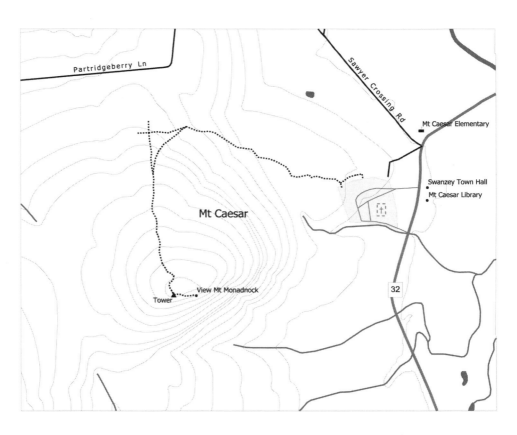

N

0   0.25 mi

THE HIKE

MT. CAESAR

To reach the trail that follows the eastern slope you must actually walk through the graveyard past the ancient headstones. Look for the Carpenter family plot in the far right hand corner. Walk to the very end of the cemetery two hundred feet to the right. This is where the trail begins on an old gravel path bordered by a stone wall on both sides. Somewhere along this path Caesar is said to have lived in a shack style home. At .3 miles the trail comes to a fork. Stay left at the fork and the summit is reached in another easy .3 miles. All in all, this is a short hike—just under a mile—taking no longer than an hour to complete. The summit offers nice views of the lake and Mt. Monadnock. Be sure to be down the mountain by dark!

From Mt. Caesar Cemetery to the summit of Mt. Caesar is approximately 1 mile.

Time:	Less than 1 hour
Parking:	Free
What to look for:	Family grave plot of Carpenter family and other historic grave stones. Also in Swanzey, four historic covered bridges and bike trail.
For more information:	Swanzey Historical Society, www.town.swanzey.nh.us

WHERE IS THIS PLACE?

The Mt. Caesar Cemetery is located across from Swanzey Town Hall on Rte. 32 in Swanzey. To get there take 101 West to Rte. 12 South, then take Rte. 32 South into Swanzey Village. Mt. Caesar Cemetery will be on the right.

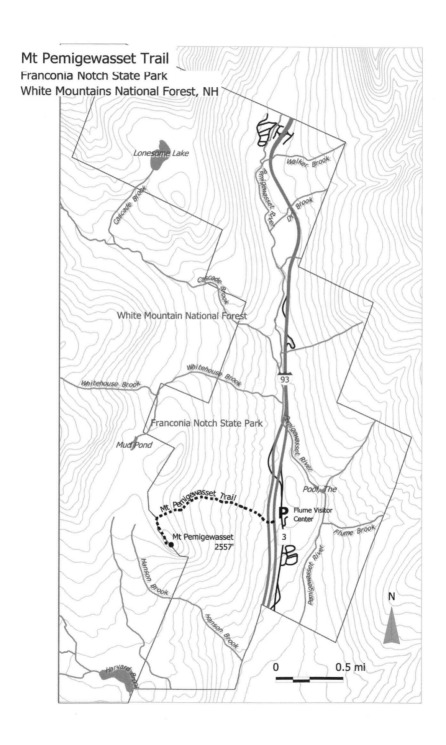

Mt Pemigewasset Trail
Franconia Notch State Park
White Mountains National Forest, NH

Indian Head and the UFO

The oldest presumed UFO photograph in history was taken on Mt. Washington in 1870. This sought-after photograph was shot over the winter of 1870–1871 on the summit. The image depicts gray, billowy cloud formations with a dark cigar-shaped object floating inside. A reflection of the object can also be seen. Over the last 130 years, the 3-D stereo image remains unexplained; it was taken long before manned aircraft was introduced. The photo remains a mystery to this day. It was auctioned off to a private company on eBay. Mysterious UFO occurrences have continued to be a part of New Hampshire's strange history with outer space. Even more bizarre is the mysterious abduction of a New Hampshire couple in Franconia Notch nearly 200 years after the first photo image of a UFO was ever taken by man.

It's been called by UFO chroniclers as "the most significant UFO sighting and abduction in UFO lore." Though the incident took place in 1961, the Hills did not openly come forward until 1966 following the release of John Fuller's retelling of the abduction in his book, *The Interrupted Journey*.

Betty and Barney Hill had taken a much needed vacation to Canada in September of 1961 when they made an early departure for home due to an impending hurricane. Driving back from Canada along the dark stretch of Rte. 3 through Franconia Notch, Betty began to notice that a bright star appeared to be following their car. Betty looked at the object through binoculars and noticed windows and flashing lights on the craft. The couple pulled their car over just south of Indian Head Resort near Mt. Pemigewasset. The place was Clark's field, an open expanse of grassy meadow along the desolate highway. Barney was then able to take a look for himself. Instantly, he was gripped by fear as he spotted a pilot and other figures watching him: he believed they would be captured. He shouted to Betty in the car, "I don't believe it!" Then, as Barney later described it, this large flashing pancake-disc moved towards him about eighty feet off the ground. Not knowing what on earth the object was, Barney tore the binoculars from his neck and ran back toward the car screaming, "We have to get out of here!" They sped from the field and tore down the road, paranoid that the disc was right on top of them. Suddenly, they were both feeling very drowsy, even amidst a growing panic of imminent danger. An odd beeping sound came from the trunk . . . they sank into a hypnotic state and soon lost all sense of time and memory.

Use lots of care with young children and dogs, when ascending Mt. Pemigewasset from either the Indian Head Trail or Mt. Pemigewasset Trail.

Betty vaguely remembered pieces of their furious escape from Clark's field: driving through North Woodstock, taking a left at Rte. 175, pulling into a dirt road . . . but then nothing. A second series of beeping noises awoke them, and the flying disc flew over them one last time. They were in Ashland, miles where they first encountered the ship. They did not fully regain consciousness until they neared Concord. Even then, they hadn't realized that hours had passed, which they couldn't account for. Both their watches had stopped. They arrived back in Portsmouth at 5:00 a.m., well beyond their predicted arrival time. Something had happened in the mountains, but neither of them could recall. Evidence of an unusual experience emerged in the form of shiny circles on their car. When Betty held a compass to the spots, the compass needle began to spin erratically. The couple quietly filed a report with the Pease Air Force base just two days after the incident. There they learned that the Pease radar system had picked up "an unknown" on the very same night. They were instructed to keep their story quiet, and for a long time, the Hills rarely spoke of the incident.

In the years that followed, both Barney and Betty experienced strange medical and psychological symptoms. Barney had an area of warts growing near his groin. They both suffered from mental exhaustion and night terrors. The couple was referred to a Boston neuro-psychiatrist, Dr. Benjamin Simon, who specialized in hypnosis. It was under hypnosis, two years after their abduction, that the Hills began to retrieve the terrifying memories of their capture, examinations, and the testing by the beings aboard the spacecraft.

Eleven beings, led by a leader dressed in black, flagged down their car near Russell Pond. The car's engine failed and the Hills were powerless under the aliens' control. They fell into an induced sleep state. Betty and Barney were then lifted into the spacecraft where a series of testing took place on their bodies and organs. Betty was told again and again by her captors that she would not be harmed. Nervously, she spoke to the aliens about food, the human life span, old age, and even dentures. She was shown a "star map" that detailed where the aliens came from. Then, with the testing complete, the Hills were escorted back to their car. In a final statement, the alien leader said to the couple, "I'm going to leave you here, why don't you stand here and watch us leave." And that is the last memory Betty was able to hold onto as the fiery, blazing craft soared off into the night sky.

Though the Hills kept quiet, the media did not, and word from Pease leaked to the press. The first headline to reveal the story was described as the "Incident at Indian Head" in 1965. A year later, John Fuller's published account of their story was released.

Even long after Barney's death in 1969, Betty stayed connected with the UFO researchers. She gave talks and lectures and spoke out about the abduction. Betty died in 2004 after a long battle with cancer. She was eighty-five. Her story and her unwavering character have convinced many that the Hill's experiences were genuine. Most incredible is Betty's visual memory of the strange "star map" she had seen in the ship. Under hypnosis, she recreated this map from visual memory. This recreated sketch of the map depicted an arrangement of stars later identified by astronomer Marjorie Fish in 1969. No other human being could possibly have created this intricate star pattern. Today it is known as the Fish-Hill Pattern.

For the unearthly visitors who came to New Hampshire during this restless period, the journey must have been provocative and educational. What did they learn from us? UFO activity in New Hampshire exists even today in small stories, which appear sporadically in regional papers. The most recent series of sightings have occurred in the Rumney–Plymouth–Tilton area. Paul Spera, a UFO hunter in Tilton, has captured videos of large triangular crafts swooping in over I-93. The crafts, he says, have become more elaborate.

For those seeking to connect with an alien experience, just stop by your local library for advice. An open mind, fearless spirit, and belief in a world outside our own is apparently all you need. The summit near Clark's field where Betty and Barney Hill first encountered the alien ship is ideal. Mt. Pemigewasset, also known as Indian Head Mountain, overlooks old Rte. 3 with an amazing panoramic vista. Below you'll see Parkers Motel, Indian Head Resort, and further south, Clark's field where the trees still stand today. On the top of Mt. Pemigewasset you can imagine their journey—the encounter that haunted their memories, and the unwavering faith that Betty Hill endured as America's first alien abductee.

Indian Head

Mt. Pemigewasset in Lincoln is named after the famous Chief Pemigewasset who used this mountain top as a lookout for enemies during the war of 1812. When the mountain was named it was entirely covered in a dense growth of trees. Then, in the early 1900s a fire swept through the region and scorched the forest that grew on the mountain top. When the smoke cleared and the ashes settled to the earth an amazing sight was revealed. An Indian head profile emerged from the remnants of the blaze. It had been there all along, underneath the trees

THE HIKE

INDIAN HEAD TRAIL, LINCOLN

The top of Mt. Pemigewasset is an ideal vantage point and affords outstanding views over Franconia Notch Parkway. The summit overlooks the area where Betty and Barney Hill first encountered the UFO back in 1961. The Indian Head Trail parking area is almost directly across the Indian Head resort. Look for a brown sign designating "Trail Head Parking" on the west side of Rte. 3. This trail runs to the summit in 1.9 miles. The trail crosses over a field then follows along a brook which runs under the overpass. It climbs moderately through hardwoods on an old logging road then meets up with the Mt. Pemigewasset Trail at 1.8 miles. The open ledges at the summit are outstanding and afford incredible views. If you have a clear day, you can see Mt. Lafayette, Lincoln, and Liberty along Franconia Ridge. Some of the ledges can be steep and slippery when wet.

MT. PEMIGEWASSET TRAIL, LINCOLN

This trail to Mt. Pemigewasset is probably the more popular trail and begins at the Flume Visitor Center, off Franconia Notch Parkway. The trail follows along the paved pedestrian bike path for 150 yards to the north of the parking lot. The trail takes a left and goes under a tunnel where Rte. 3 crosses above. After crossing a small bridge it then goes under the Parkway. At .4 miles the trail enters the woods and crosses several bridges. At 1.3 miles look for a large boulder to pass around. Here the trail begins a steep climb toward the summit. At 1.7 miles, it meets at a junction with the Indian Head Trail and soon reaches the summit at 1.8 miles. This trail to the summit can also be slippery and dangerous when wet. Use lots of care with young children and dogs when ascending Mt. Pemigewasset from either the Indian Head Trail or Mt. Pemigewasset Trail. My dog almost slipped over this steep cliff ledge chasing a squirrel on the top of the Indian's forehead.

Indian Head facts:

Actual measurements of the Indian Head's features:
- 98 vertical feet from forehead to chin
- 17 feet vertical across the forehead
- 42 feet along the nose
- 23 feet along the upper lip
- 16 feet down the chin. The top of the forehead is
    1,330' above Rte. 3

Mt. Pemigewasset summit via both Indian Head Trail and Mt. Pemigewasset Trail, approximately 2-mile moderate/challenging hike.

Time:	3-4 hours round trip.
Parking:	Free.
What to look for:	Views from the top, Indian head features, UFOs. Pemigewasset Trail, parking fee. Public restrooms and facilities available at Flume Visitor Center.
Contact:	AMC (603)466-2727
Flume Gorge Visitor center:	603-745-8391

WHERE IS THIS PLACE?

To get there take I-93 north to exit 33 off Interstate 93. Follow signs to the Indian Head Rock Profile and Indian Head Resort. This puts you on Rte. 3. Trailhead parking is located 1.4 miles north on Rte. 3 on the left hand side. Flume Visitor Center is located off the Franconia Parkway at exit 34A.

Indian Head Mt.

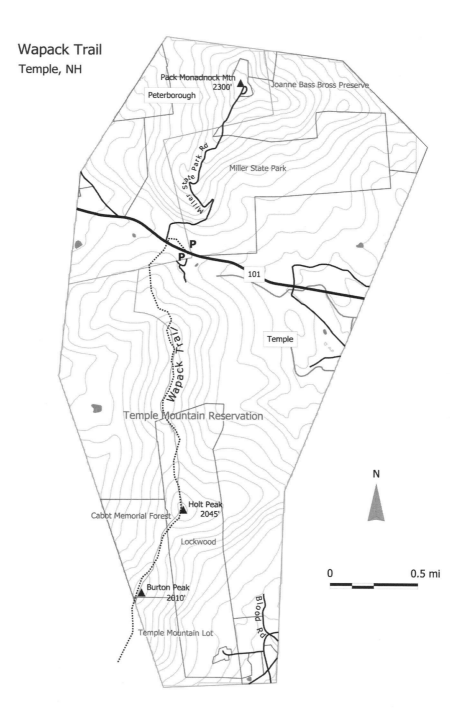

Wapack Trail
Temple, NH

Pack Monadnock Mtn
2300'

Joanne Bass Bross Preserve

Peterborough

Miller State Park Rd

Miller State Park

P

P

101

Temple

Wapack Trail

Temple Mountain Reservation

N

Holt Peak
2045'

Cabot Memorial Forest

Lockwood

Burton Peak
2010'

Blood Rd

Temple Mountain Lot

0   0.5 mi

5 Temple's Sitting Spirits

Temple Mountain rises in the western part of town along the ridge of the Wapack Mountain range. Its highest point, Holt peak, is only 2,055 feet. This area was once a ski resort, and visitors will see the remnants of this once prosperous business in the abandoned buildings crumbling in deterioration. Miller State park receives lots of visitors, and is just across the way along the Wapack Range. But there is something unique about Temple Mountain, something that makes this small peak a must for mystery lovers and ghost hunters. The mountain is just a few short miles from the Temple town village. This small town lists a population of only 1,500, and though the town itself is tiny, those who visit can't help but be lured back by its charm and country magic. There's the town hall and Willard's Country Store located centrally in town. The pinnacle is the Birchwood Inn, operating as a public hotel since 1775. Henry David Thoreau even stayed at the Birchwood. He too was enchanted by its rural mystique and character.

As in most small towns, there are stories and forbidden secrets. And though the locals enjoy a bit of gossip now and then, there are some secrets too painful to discuss even to this day, such as the death of Freida Hedman back in the Great Depression.

Frieda was the postmaster in Temple, a wife and mother of three grown children. Rumors in town began when the small store and post office operated by the Hedman family came under scrutiny by authorities regarding missing monies. Rather than face the pain and anguish her family would face if indicted, Freida took her own life on October of 1932. She left behind a grieving family, including her daughter, Anna, who would be plagued by tragedy throughout her life.

Near the time of her mother's death, Anna's father bought the Birchwood Inn across the street in the town common. For Anna, who had known only sadness and despair in her young life, the inn became an escape. Here she could watch young couples dance in the ballroom and become lost in the bustle of busy hotel life. She immersed herself with kitchen chores and laughed and danced at the parties her father coordinated. Anna had a flare for the business and created brochures advertising the inn as a perfect get away for skiers and hikers.

Anna became engaged to a young piano player, Larry Hill, and they were married. They soon took over the business of running the inn throughout the 1940s and WWII. But tragedy struck. Larry was walking home from Peterborough one night when he was struck by a hit-and-run driver and killed. The accident was never solved. After Larry Hill's death, Anna married Joe Aurichio, and they ran the inn for several more years before selling it to the Turrini family in 1964. According to the Turrinis, Anna often opened up the inn for traveling hikers from the AMC. After Joe's death, she lived in Florida, traveling up to New Hampshire periodically. Anna died on October 14, 1984, almost fifty-two years to the day that her mother died. She is buried locally in Miller Cemetery.

Throughout her life, Anna Hedman-Aurichio maintained a deep connection with the inn, and even lived there for a period in the backyard in a small house. When the Turrinis sold the inn to Bill and Judy Wolfe, Anna was a frequent visitor. "Can I come in and sit at the parlor," she would shyly ask Bill. Bill would chuckle. Of course

she could, she was always a welcome to sit on the porch or in the parlor for as long as she wished. Later in her life, it is all she seemed to want to do and she could be seen at the inn several times a week. But she was never a bother. She simply sat and watched, perhaps glancing sadly at the little store where her mother ended her life. Despite her losses, the inn offered her the comfort of cherished memories and happy times.

If you decide to visit the Birchwood Inn, you might be tempted to sit and relax awhile. But be careful where you sit—the seats at the Birchwood are sometimes occupied by ghosts!

Much before Anna's time, the Birchwood Inn also had its share of misfortunate and even macabre events. During the 1890s, the Inn was known as the Old Hotel, and kept a number of transient boarders who moved in and out of the area. Drifters, railroad workers, and other out of town guests frequented the Old Hotel. A young bride came to the Birchwood with a male guest, all under a cloud of suspicion. The woman was married to a minister. She had begun an illicit affair with her husband's friend and the two had planned a romantic getaway. Naturally, the minister grew suspicious when both his friend and his wife were "out of town" at the same time. The woman told her husband she was visiting a cousin out of state. But the minister began to put the pieces together and he rode out to Temple believing his wife might be there. She had always reminisced about the beautiful mountain scenery in Temple, and the minister was following a hunch. When he arrived at the hotel he asked if his friend had been checked in as a guest. When told that he had, the minister asked to see the woman who had accompanied him. Hidden in his coat sleeve, the minister had a loaded pistol. When the woman came to the head of the stairs, he saw that it was in fact his wife. In a sudden blast that shook the whole town, he shot his wife and she collapsed and fell down the flight of stairs, dead.

When Bill Wolf purchased the Inn, he began an expansion to include home-cooked meals in the kitchen. Breakfast was served everyday to guests and local residents alike. During the 1980s Bill began receiving peculiar reports from his overnight guests. "This sounds weird," they'd tell him, "but a woman came into my room at night and sat in a chair." At first Bill dismissed the reports, but over the years more and more guests said the same thing to Bill and his wife Judy. Some waited until they were miles away from the inn before calling. They all said the same thing: each encounter with the unknown woman occurred at night when all others were asleep. The guest would be aware of someone entering the room and leaving the door open. Some thought it was the innkeeper "checking up" on them. But when they looked over, they saw an old woman in a blue dress sitting in a chair. The woman would gaze upon the sleeping guest and then get up and move along. Over and over Bill heard these stories, though he himself never saw a thing. One day a guest happened to snap a photo in the dining room during a visit, and there in the picture was the woman in the blue dress. Her image was clear, sitting among the dining guests at the Birchwood. To Bill it only made reasonable sense that the spirit was that of Anna Hedman, but others believe it was the woman shot by her husband at the top of the stairway. Some, like Jim Haddix, author of the town's history, don't believe Anna Hedman was the ghost "type," but there are many in town who do.

The woman would gaze upon the sleeping guest and then get up and move along.

The Birchwood is under new management, and to this day reports of unusual circumstances are well known. When the new owners refurbished the building, new framed paintings went into all the bedrooms. The ghost apparently disapproved of these new paintings, and one by one they fell from the walls. When the electricians and plumbers hammered on the interior walls, someone banged back in protest. The kitchen staff, a group of young men, reported that someone had been tickling their ears while they worked in the kitchen. (The kitchen staff, still report that.)

On the other end of town, along the Wapack Trail, there is another popular sitting spot for hikers. Just below the summit of Temple Mountain's Holt Peak there is a cluster of granite chairs. These furnishings include about eight pieces of furniture designed to resemble armchairs, recliners, and other living room décor. Further along, hidden behind low lying bushes, are several other artistic cairns. These cairns appeared on the Wapack years ago and no one can say for certain who built them or when. But this historic section of the Wapack has ties to the original Wapack trail builders. You could take a break along the hike and relax at the site of these mysterious cairns. It's the perfect spot for lunch and offers some views over to the Monadnock Valley. But once again, you'll want to check before you sit down. According to legend, these granite chairs are also inhabited by spirits!

The history tied with these Wapack Mountains begins with the first woman trailblazer in New Hampshire: Marion Buck Davis. In 1922, Marion Buck and Frank Robbins worked on their dream: a twenty-two mile long trail through wooded forests and meadows and up over several rocky mountain summits. The Wapack Trail is one of the oldest interstate trails in the Northeast. The trail begins in Ashburnham, Massachusetts, and ends at Old Mountain Road in Greenfield, New Hampshire. As mountaineering trampers, Marion and Frank envisioned a public access trail that would someday connect these low lying mountains to the "friends" that cared about them most. As a child, Marion grew up poor. At one point, her father moved the family to Panama where he worked constructing shelters

The kitchen staff, a group of young men, reported that someone had been tickling their ears while they worked in the kitchen. (The kitchen staff still report that.)

for the Panama Canal work crews. Marion had been a feisty and independent "tomboy" all her life. She loved the outdoors and her favorite sport was hockey. As a teen she left her family to live on a farm in Rindge, New Hampshire. It was here that she met Frank Robbins. The two nature enthusiasts envisioned a trail and set out to make it happen. In one year they devoted most days to blazing trails and chopping brush, and then they fell in love. They married in 1946 and spent years welcoming hikers and skiers to their rustic Wapack Lodge in New Ipswich. It was Marion who actually named the trail "Wapack," which combined the first syllable of the first mountain peak, Mt. Watatic, to the last peak, Pack Monadnock— hence Wapack. Marion also came up with the idea for the trail blaze: the yellow triangle. These triangles follow the trail the entire twenty-two miles through two states and represent friendship. Marion died in 1988 and the lodge she built with her husband Frank burned down in a terrible fire. More than anything, Marion's greatest joy in life was being part of the outdoor world and connecting new friends to these sacred places. She was known as a gracious hostess and diligent tour guide.

After the fire destroyed the Wapack lodge, the number of visitors to this area has declined somewhat. Heavier boot traffic can be found across Rte. 101 at Miller State Park where the Marion Davis Trail and the Wapack Trail climb to the most popular peak on the entire trail:

Pack Monadnock. But Temple Mountain still maintains its charm as a quiet place to hike. An ambitious effort has been underway to save it from future development. The pristine beauty and quiet serenity on the trail is a place for reflection, and long ago, the old time trampers who hiked through these parts thought the same.

As the summit marks the boundary lines between Sharon and Temple, stone cairns were designated as town boundary markers. Over the last fifty years though, something odd has happened. These granite structures, created from loose rocks, are often used in the place of trail blazes when there are no trees around. The mountain has always had its share of cairns, and there are several along the trail that lead to Holt peak. Over time, these cairns have begun to take the shape of chairs, chaise lounges, and sofas. Other decorative and artistic cairns showed up both on and off the trail. The chairs simply "happened" without anyone knowing who contributed to their design and structure. The Friends of the Wapack jokingly refer to them as ancient ruins left by the Druids. But perhaps their significance ties in with the legend of Marion Davis and Frank Robbins.

Long ago, this portion of the trail was much more scenic, but it has since grown in over the years. As daytime hikers reached this point, they have an unusual spot to enjoy the views of the Monadnock Valley and beyond. But at night, so they say, the spirits of these early trampers and trailblazers return to Temple Mountain to reflect upon their earthly existence. There are enough stone chairs to go around, and the old friends can rekindle the flames that united them in life. Frank and Marion always have a reservation on Temple, no matter how crowded.

Another ghost story has circulated around this little town: Back in 1777, at the old Rockwood House, four children were standing on a porch watching a lightning storm. A stream of lightning struck a beam and electrocuted two of the children, Hannah and Jack Searle, ages ten and twelve, respectively. They were killed instantly. Occasionally, if you drive by the house, folks say that can see the shadows of the two children gazing out from the attic windows. The former owners of the house say they often heard voices of children laughing and crying.

Friends of the Wapack are a volunteer group that helps to maintain trails. www.wapack.org

THE HIKE

TEMPLE MOUNTAIN

The hike to Temple Mountain (elevation 2,045') is a moderate 2.4 mile hike up the yellow triangle-blazed Wapack trail to the highest point, Holt Peak. You will pass through the vacant Temple Mountain Ski Area. Look for the memorial bench dedicated to Mr. and Mrs. Beebe who ran the ski area until its closing in 2001. Be on the lookout for a mysterious cairn along the first rise; this rock formation "points" to where the chairs can be found, just off-trail. They are obscured by brush and are not entirely visible from the trail. Holt Peak is only a short distance from here, and further south at another half mile is Burton Peak which has nice views to the west.

From Temple Mt. parking area to Holt Peak it is a moderate 2.4-mile hike to summit via Wapack Trail.

Time:	Allow 2–3 hours for exploration
Parking at Temple	Currently no fee, but may change
What to look for:	Amazing views over Monadnock Valley toward Mt. Monadnock. Wild Blueberries, perfect for picking late July-August seasonally. Creative cairn structures and sitting spirits.
Contact:	www.wapack.org
Birchwood Inn contact:	www.thebirchwoodinn.com (603)878-3285 open year round

WHERE IS THIS PLACE?

The Temple Mountain State Reservation is located on the border of Peterborough and Temple in the Monadnock Region.

Take Rte. 101 West through to the town of Temple. At the Peterborough town line, look for the old Temple Mt. Ski Area. Park in the gravel lot. Follow the old dirt road off to the right of the parking lot and look for the yellow triangle blazes. The Wapack Trail picks up from here and is clearly blazed.

The Birchwood Inn is located on Rte. 45 South, four miles east of Temple Mt. To get there, take Rte. 101 traveling east to the junction of Rte. 45, then follow 45 South to Temple Center.

6 Devil's Den: Chasing Satan!

High on the cliffs of Mt. Willard in Crawford Notch is Devil's Den, a dark abyss beyond the trail line and beneath the cliffs. Ethan Allen Crawford was spooked by what he saw in the mouth of the cavern: a litter of human skeletal remains. Other hikers explored the mouth and one, a climber named Leavitt, was left queasy and trembling at the sight and could not muster the tenacity to search the cavern further.

> *When the devil left town, he left his footprints on Sandwich Notch Road.*

But in the 1870s a new surveying group bravely entered the den. They found no sign that the bones had ever been there. Satan had already moved on. (From *The White Mountain Scrap Book: Early Stories and Legends of the Crystal Hills*, by Ernest Bisbee.)

Satan traveled to the North Country where the Devil's Hop yard appears, a rocky gorge in the Kilkenney Mountain Range. Another remote path leads to Devil's Slide in the northern section of Stark Village. Hell's Gate is found along the Bearcamp River Trail in South Tamworth. The narrow gorge was once a difficult pass for log drivers. Today, it's a challenge for kayakers. When the devil left town, he left his footprints on Sandwich Notch Road.

In the Lakes Region there is another Devil's Den Mountain. At only 1,110 feet, it's hardly a mountain at all. Located just outside New Durham Village, this rocky hill is an easy scramble to the top. From the summit, gaze upon the shimmering waters of Lake Winnipesauke near Rattlesnake Island. An unmarked path leads to interesting geological features and secret hideaway coves. The panorama overlooking the lake is incredible. Even the devil enjoys the views from the top.

Devils Den Trail - Devils Den Cave

New Durham, NH

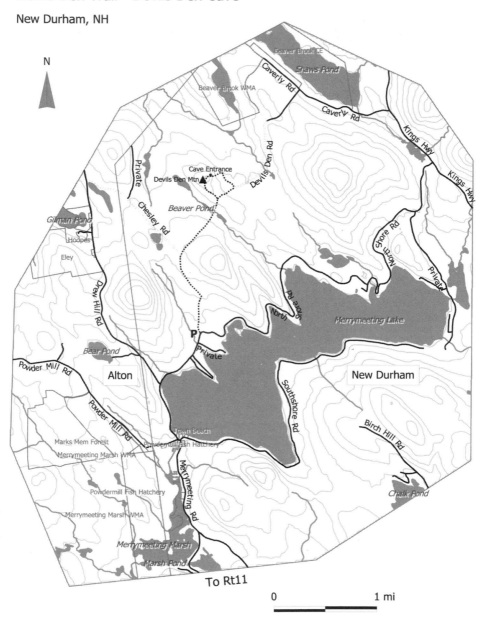

THE HIKE

DEVIL'S DEN

When packing for this trip, bring strong boots or sneakers, gloves, headlamps, and flashlights.

The trick in finding the route to Devil's Den requires knowing exactly how to get there. New Durham Road leaves Rte. 11 at the rotary in Alton where Rte. 11 and Rte. 28 merge. Follow New Durham Road for one mile, and when it turns into Main St., take a left onto Merrymeeting Lake Road where there's a sign for the Fish Hatchery. Follow along this road where the lake is on the right. The road is recently paved but very narrow. At four miles this road abruptly ends and North Shore Road comes in at the right. There is a dirt road straight ahead where the paved road ends. This is the route that takes you to the Devil's Den Mt. Trailhead. The rough dirt road is not passable for most cars unless you have an off-road vehicle. Don't attempt to drive it. Even though it looks passable, there are steep pitches and large rocks waiting to do damage. Pull over to the left to park; there is a small clearing almost as soon as you enter the dirt road. The road is used by ATVs, so be on the look out. In summer the road side is lined with raspberry bushes and lady slippers. They grow abundantly along both sides of the road.

Next follow the dirt road until the fork at .8 miles. Bear right, and hike past a beaver pond on the left at 1.3 miles. After the beaver pond the road rises to a height of land at 1.5 miles. After the road rises, look to your left for a faintly marked trailhead. There is a rock with a faded arrow. From here, the trail is fairly obvious. Notice the red blazes on the trees that lead you past an old stone wall. The trail swings right and has fairly moderate grades. At once you'll notice the large boulder and rock formations on the right. There is a whole network of other trails in here, so if you decide to reach the small summit by scrambling over theses ledges, be sure you remember which way you came. The main trail soon reaches the small summit at 1.8 miles. At the top, there are pretty good views of Winnipesaukee to the north and Merrymeeting Lake to the south. Suddenly, you realize you are standing on steep cavernous ledges! Below, the furrows have scoured deep into this granite surface by ancient glaciers. You will notice grooves where boulders were trapped under ice. Look for pits and holes within the ledges from pocket weathering.

Then the fun begins. Here is where headlamps come in handy, allowing free use of your hands, which you'll need as you enter the cave and scout around. The mouth of the den is just below the summit. From the summit, go all the way over the top and back down again following the trail. The trail takes a fork. Take the right at the first junction. Then, a left turn at another fork in the trail. Before turning left, you will notice a gaping hole in a boulder—that is the ceiling of Devil's Den, and you can actually climb out to the Den's rooftop by ladder from below. Here you will scramble over some tricky rock piles. Follow the trail to the left. Graffiti mark the cave's spooky entrance and the opening is

Only the brave dare enter Devil's Den cave!

about six feet in height, but once inside, you need to do some crouching and maneuvering over rock and ledge. The cave is also cold and damp, so if you're even the slightest bit claustrophobic, this might not be the thing for you. The cave continues deep into the mountain for twenty feet and a ladder can be seen which you can climb if you are slender enough to fit into the tiny crack allowing access to it. There are a lot of markings on the walls from all the visitors who have come to explore this cavern. Some folks say they have seen remnants of blood on the walls and have heard the echoes of terrified shrieking. You might feel a sharp prodding against your side while clambering through the cave. No, it's not the sharp, jutting rocks poking your ribs. It's Satan inviting you down a bottomless passage for eternal cave exploration!

Devil's Den summit is approximately 1.9 miles on unnamed trail/red blazes. Easy to moderate hike over gravel road to trailhead turn off.

Time:	Allow 2-3 hours for both hiking and cave exploration.
What to look for:	Is there blood on the walls of the interior cave? Beaver pond along road has frogs and other wildlife. Raspberries grow abundantly along roadside in August.
Parking:	No parking fee.
For more information:	Merrymeeting Lake Association www.mmlake.org

Ammonoosuc Ravine Trail
to Lakes of the Clouds Hut
White Mountains National Forest, NH

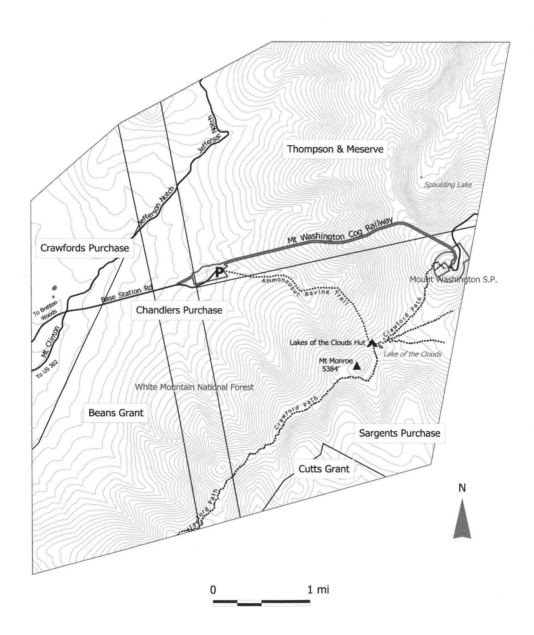

7 Haunted Huts on the Highest Peaks

I n New Hampshire's White Mountains there are eight high mountain huts offering welcome shelter and cozy stops for hikers. The stone hut structure deep in the woods of Carter Notch is haunted by the benevolent spirit of Milton MacGregor. The ghost is known to pay surprise visits to hut caretakers and campers alike.

Only in New Hampshire will you find the unique feature of the Appalachian Mountain Club's (AMC) high mountain hut system. The first of these sturdy lodges appeared in the higher peaks of the Presidential Mountain range in a shoulder between Mt. Adams and Mt. Madison. Madison Spring Hut was constructed of stone in the year 1888. And in 1914, the construction of Carter Notch Hut was underway,

The Lakes of the Clouds Hut is also haunted, but the spirits that visit that are neither benevolent nor kind.

replacing an old log cabin the mountaineers used as a camp and shelter. Joe Dodge is the pioneer and visionary credited with establishing the system of connected huts, which are popular among hikers to this day. Carter Notch Hut is the oldest and Mizpah Springs Hut is the most recent.

The Lakes of the Clouds Hut was built in 1915, fourteen years after the creation of an emergency shelter at the same spot. The oldest trail to Mt. Washington, blazed by Abel Crawford and his son Ethan in 1819, passes by Bigelow Lawn. Before the building of this hut, just below the summit of Mt. Washington, an emergency shelter was erected after two experienced mountain men perished in a ferocious storm in the summer in 1900. The Lakes of the Clouds Hut is also haunted, but the spirits that visit that hut are neither benevolent nor kind.

Alan Ormsbee, who died tragically on June 30, 1900, along with his partner William Curtis, may be two of the spirits that haunt the highest summit in the northeast. But so many men and women have lost their lives on the mountain top that no one can ever say for sure. Even the bravest of hut caretakers wouldn't dare spend a night alone in the Lake of the Clouds Hut. The Presence in the summit house buildings is truly terrifying.

Mt. Washington Weather Observatory and Lakes of the Clouds Hut

The poltergeist and the frightening specters that have been seen upon the summit of Mt. Washington and the nearby Lakes of the Clouds Hut have left even the most fearless of AMC crew members shaking and terrified. Scientists and meteorologists at the weather observatory admit witnessing dark shadows ("corner cats"), but say they are all just a trick of the mind. But there have been other reports of strange happenings at the weather observatory, which is manned throughout the year. It has been said that the toilets flush by themselves, and the elevator doors open and close on their own. Peter Crane, at the station, says that most of the phenomena can be explained. The "corner cats" are shadows that seem to slink around the corners and out of sight, like black cats seen out of the corner of the eye. "It's a psychological phenomenon. You think you see something, but it's really not there at all. And that can be pretty spooky."

Mt. Washington has claimed the lives of over 130 people. In *Not Without Peril*, Nicholas Howe relates the unforgiving weather conditions on the mountain, and the toll on the men and women, some of them young teenagers, who tragically lost their lives over the last 150 years. One such tale concerns two climbers from New York in 1900. William Curtis, 63, and Alan Ormsbee, 29, were caught in a raging snow and sleet storm on June 30th, as they attempted to reach the Summit Hotel by way of the Crawford Path. The two never made it. Fighting blasts of arctic winds and dangerous ice covered rocks on the exposed trail, the men were two miles from the safety of the hotel's quarters when they both succumbed to the elements. The violent storm raged on for three days before searchers could safely begin the efforts to recover the bodies. The body of William Curtis was discovered first on Bigelow

Lawn, near where the Lakes of the Clouds hut stands today, his head resting on a rock. Just ahead of him, Ormsbee's body was found covered in lacerations, bruises, and scratches, as he had possibly made a final attempt to get help. His body was recovered on Mt. Washington's cone, just yards from the summit where he would have found shelter.

A year after the two men were found dead, an emergency shelter was constructed near the very spot where Curtis had perished. Additionally, a wooden cross marks the site where Ormsbee was found, and a bronze plaque memorialized the site for Curtis. It was placed by the New York Fresh Air Club. The plaque placed where Curtis's body was recovered, however, didn't stay put. What was happening with the plaque? In one version of events, the plaque itself was powered by supernatural energies. By forces unknown, the plaque mysteriously tore itself loose from the boulder where it was secured, and blew along the lawn and landed at the Lakes of the Clouds doorway. This happened more than once, as the story goes. Work crews would trudge out to the boulder and again re-secure the plaque, but each time, it removed itself from the boulder, apparently finding a more desirable location in front of the hut. The last efforts to secure the plaque have been successful. It is bolted tightly inside the crew room at the Lakes of the Clouds. The plaque is finally satisfied, perhaps, that some form of Curtis and his final fatal trek to shelter has been accomplished.

The story of Curtis and Ormsbee is a somber reminder that even in summer, the mountain is capable of turning on even the most skilled climbers and mountaineers. In the years that followed, the AMC has worked diligently with its members to focus on safety for members and visitors to the Presidential Range. Some AMC crew members have even gone so far as to demonstrate bravado and admonishment in their discussions of the two fallen hikers from New York. The debate over whether the men should have turned back in the foul weather or persevered as they did still carries on in some circles. In a reconstruction of the events, it appears that Bill went down first, exhausted and overcome. Ormsbee may have created a makeshift shelter from brush and vegetation for Curtis. But for some reason, Curtis seems to have left this area and gone ahead, maybe to try and catch his friend.

It is protocol among some crew members that the utmost respect be paid to Ormsbee and Curtis, though some self-righteous hikers demonstrate otherwise. One story tells of a crew member who jokingly mocked Ormsbee's failed efforts to survive the "Storm of the Century." As the hiker passed by the wooden cross bearing Ormsbee's name at his death site, the man scorned the two by shouting out, "Those idiots should have turned back when the storm started!" No sooner had the last syllable been uttered from his mouth when a force so powerful struck him like an iron fist to his chest and knocked him over backward. The lesson quickly passed among AMC staff: when passing Ormsbee's cross, it is best to remark upon the strength and heroic perseverance as well as the dreadful bad luck that befell the two men. "It could have happened to anyone," is the safest chant for crew members to say in passing.

In another Lakes of the Clouds Hut tale, an AMC crew member named George was sent up in the spring with a two-way radio to assess the winter damage and report back to the crew below any special equipment that might be needed for opening the hut. As in every winter, with the north winds blowing so fiercely, the windows of the hut are boarded up tight and secure. This was just how George found them that day. By the afternoon, the men at the base signaled up to the lone hiker to see that he had made a safe arrival. Strangely, he did not answer. This didn't worry the other members of the crew at first. Maybe he had gone out for a little hike around to check on some other things. By 8:00 that evening, the crew tried again and still there was no radio response from George. Anxiety rose, and the members at the base drew out a plan for an early morning exodus to the hut to check on their friend's safety.

The hut was eerily dark with the windows still boarded up from the harsh winter. Someone heard a noise . . .

The next morning they made their way, slow and steady up the snow-packed trail to the hut. From all indications, George had arrived safely at the hut: his backpack and gear lay opened on the dining room floor. There on a table was his two-way radio, still powered. They called out for him, but couldn't find him anywhere. The searchers began looking outside for footprints; they looked in the bunkrooms with their flashlights and headlamps. The hut was eerily dark with the windows still boarded up from the harsh winter. Someone heard a noise—a whimper, coming from below the kitchen sink. At last George was found, shaking horribly, and crouched under the sink with the cabinet doors closed. In his white fists he clutched an axe, and he pleaded with his crew mates, "Just please, get me the hell out of here. Just get me out of here!"

Stunned by this discovery, the crew members quickly pulled him out of the cupboard. He was soaked in sweat and trembling in fear. The members begged George to tell them what was wrong, yet he would not answer them. He simply repeated, "Just get me the hell out of here! Please!" Quietly, they surrounded their friend in a secure clutch and helped him outside the hut and back onto the trail down the

Suddenly, he felt as if there was someone else in the large dining room with him.

mountain. One crew member radioed back to the Pinkham Notch base for assistance and an ambulance was waiting for them as soon as they reached the bottom.

What terror had taken form at the hut to reduce this bravest of men into a state of unprecedented fear? No one could say. They guessed that he had run into a wild animal, maybe a wolf or bear, and had become fearful for his life. As the weeks passed and George lay recovering in his hospital, he finally opened up to a close confidant and relayed this story:

After his long trek up the trail, he was overcome with exhaustion and hunger. He unlocked the heavy padlocks on the hut doors and quickly went inside into the large dining hall. There he sat on a bench by one of the tables and began to take account of his food supplies as he rested. He thought he'd just wait a short while and catch his breath before radioing back to the base. Suddenly, he felt as if there was someone else in the large dining room with him. He felt a form approach him from behind, as if someone was about to put their hands on his shoulders. He jumped up and quickly turned around to face the back of the dining room hall. There, peering in at him through the dining room window was a face: a distorted, grotesque face pressed to the glass of the dining room window panes, which were entirely boarded up from the outside. George backed up in horror as he then looked at each window pane covered by the thick boards, and there he saw, one after the other, the same face, in every window, glaring back at him. Then face seemed to melt through the glass and into the room where he was standing. That was the last thing George remembered. He would never return to the hut or to the AMC crew again, and has since lost all memory of the traumatic event on the summit that changed his life forever.

The Ghost at Carter Notch Hut—Red Mac

During the 1970s, the AMC made a bold decision to keep some of the high mountain huts open through the winter months. The hut caretaker would be on shift from October straight through April. Back in those days, winter hiking in the White Mountains wasn't nearly as popular as it is now. For one, the temperatures in the bunk houses are extremely cold, sometimes dropping to double digits below zero. It was common for these early caretakers to go days and even weeks without seeing a single soul on the mountain trails. With no electricity or telephone, these hardy men were the toughest of the tough in both mind and spirit. Only the rugged need apply to the position of winter caretaker.

In the early years that the huts first operated around 1916, one of the first managers was Milton MacGregor, more commonly known as "Red Mac." Red spent most of his life as a pioneering mountain man, rugged outdoors enthusiast, and reliable friend of the trampers, who were just beginning their quests of conquering the highest peaks in the White Mountains. Even women, clad in Eskimo mukluks, could be seen traversing the peaks on Madison, Washington, and Adams. Early hikers armed themselves with rifles for protection from the "wild men" and beasts who roamed the wilderness. Red Mac was nearly shot by a couple of gun-toting ladies on the summit of Jefferson. In his later years, Red Mac let his friends and family know that his heaven would always be by the lakes in the deep forest of Carter Notch. It was a magical place that would beckon him, even after his death.

Over the winter of 1976, Joe Gill was the Carter Notch hut manager who worked the long cold winter. Alone in the hut one March night, Joe awoke with a start. As he lay on his bunk he heard the doors of the hut burst open letting the frigid windy air inside.

Nineteen Mile Brook Trail
Carter Notch Hut & Carter Dome
White Mountains National Forest
Pinkham Notch, NH

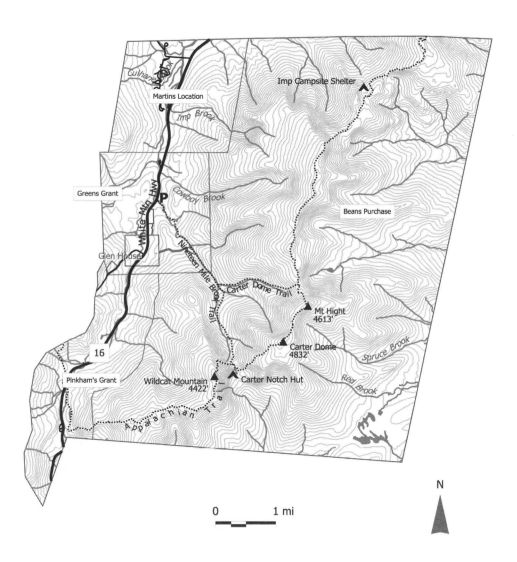

0   1 mi

N

"What inconsiderate person would allow all this cold air into the hut?" he wondered. As he pulled the blankets tightly around him, he was aware of an intensely bright light shining into his eyes. There seemed to be a shadowy figure there holding a flashlight, but the light was too bright to detect who it was. He called out, "Who is it? Can I help you?" But there was no answer.

Joe rustled about and located a headlamp he kept close by. When he put the light on he looked around the room. There was no one there. The shadowy figure was gone and instead he saw his own flashlight across the room, turned on and shining in his face. Funny, Joe thought, he hadn't left his flashlight there, and he wouldn't have left the light turned on. He got up from his warm blankets and walked the short distance of the room to shut the flashlight off again. Once he was up he checked the main room of the hut and saw that the front door had blown open. The door to the crew room was open as well. But both doors opened in opposite directions. How could that happen? For both the doors to open into the main dining area of the hut, the wind would have to be blowing out from the secure crew room where Joe slept. And that just wasn't the case. It was completely illogical. Joe wondered about the mystery, but once he checked around the building, he went back to bed and fell asleep.

Carter Hut, ca. 1914/1915. Courtesy of AMC Library, Boston.

Joe had a few days off at the end of the week and he walked down the long Nineteen-Mile Brook Trail over to the Pinkham Notch Visitor's Center. As he talked with other AMC crew members, he mentioned the unusual activity at Carter Notch Hut during his last week. As far as Joe could tell, no one ever showed up during March, but he couldn't shake that indelible feeling that someone was with him in the crew room that night holding his own flashlight.

Then one of the Center's employees spoke up: "When did you say this happened, Joe?"

Joe told him the date, March 21, 1976, and the man replied, "That was the night Red Mac died."

Red's good natured sense of humor, even in spirit, is replayed again and again as the different hut caretakers report strange happenings high in the Carter Notch Hut. Campers have heard the sounds of trampling boots on the hut's roof, or have seen the ghostly glow of a lantern deep in the woods off the beaten trail. When the crew members search for an identity, or a hiker that has passed through, there is no sign of life.

Campers have heard the sounds of trampling boots on the hut's roof, or have seen the ghostly glow of a lantern deep in the woods off the beaten trail

In the late '90s the winter hut caretaker, Bryan Yeaton, was close to finishing his shift at Carter Notch. It had been a stormy winter with copious snowfall, and he'd been isolated for weeks without a single hiker. Bryan knew the legend of Red Mac, but he was also one who was not easily spooked. Having stayed at the hut through other winters he felt safe. One afternoon while he sat reading by the fire, Bryan heard the familiar sound of heavy boots approaching the hut entrance doors, followed by the stomping sound of a hiker kicking the snow off. Bryan prepared for the hut's doors to swing open and the winter hiker to join him, but the doors remained closed. For about an hour, Bryan sat and waited for the hiker to enter the hut's main dining room. As the afternoon sun began to fade, Bryan decided to investigate, wondering why the hiker may have turned back at the door. He donned his jacket and gloves and slowly opened the hut door to peek outside. There was nothing but the sight of fresh fallen snow without a footprint in sight. Still Bryan pressed on to search the area of the bunk rooms and the lake. The half-mile walk around the edge of the lake revealed only one set of prints in the snow . . . his own.

Carter Notch Hut still operates on a self-service basis through the long, dark winter months. It's been thirty years since Red's death. Thanks to the AMC, the hut in his beloved mountains is still available for those who brave the winter weather and enjoy the company of a friendly ghost.

THE HIKE

NINETEEN-MILE BROOK TRAIL TO CARTER NOTCH HUT (3,300')

The Nineteen-Mile Brook Trail head is located in Pinkham Notch, and Parking is located on Rte. 16, 1 mile north of the Mt. Washington Auto Road. The trail follows the northeast bank of the Nineteen-Mile Brook on an old gravel road. The trail ascends at a gradual level over wide rocky path. At 1.9 miles the Carter Dome Trail diverges to the left. There is a brook crossing (footbridge) at 2.2 miles, it crosses another brook (footbridge). Here the trail climbs more steeply, to 3.6 miles; the Wildcat Ridge Trail diverges right. The Nineteen-Mile brook Trail then descends steeply to Carter Lake then passes the Carter-Moriah Trail. The trail crosses between the Lakes reaching the hut at 3.8 miles. Approximate time is 3 hours.

Additional hiking routes may be accessed from the carter Notch Hut. After your visit to the hut, and seeing the welcoming photo of Red Mac in the entry way, you can pursue higher summits from this point.

TO CARTER DOME (4,832') VIA CARTER-MORIAH TRAIL

This trail begins at the Shore of Carter Lake .1 mile north of the hut. From Carter Notch Hut, follow the Nineteen-Mile Brook Trail to the junction of the Carter Moriah Trail (.1 mile). The trail climbs very steeply, then moderates. The trail reaches the summit of Carter Dome in 1.2 miles. Though the summit is grown in with trees, there are excellent view points along the way. Approximate time is 1 hour, 25 minutes.

These Boots Were Made for Walking—
Lakes of the Clouds Hut

B en Campbell was in his twenties, vibrant and full of life, in the 1970s. He had become hut manager for the Greenleaf Hut along the famous Franconia Ridge near Mt. Lafayette, and though he was incredibly fulfilled at this station, he secretly desired to be named hut manager for the Lakes of the Clouds hut.

One summer Ben, his parents, and his brothers and sisters took a family trip to Scotland to trace their genealogy. The vacation included lots of hiking over cliffs and mountains. One cool windy day the family went climbing and Ben lost his footing, falling to his death. The family was inconsolable. They returned to the U.S. from their trip, left with the task of burying the young man whose life was cut too short. Ben's mother and father knew how much the Greenleaf Hut meant to their son. As a token, the Campbell's brought Ben's old hiking boots up to Greenleaf Hut where they hoped the boots could be left as a memorial to their son. Soon after, crew members at the hut began hearing thumping sounds in the night. In the morning they found the boots at the other end of the hut. The boots were walking themselves up and down the halls of the hut almost as if they were trying to escape. The crew members were spooked. They didn't want to give the boots back to the family, but what do you do with a pair of boots that won't stand still? Finally, it was decided to send the boots over to the Lakes of the Clouds hut. After all, this is where Campbell truly wanted to be. This time the boots would have no chance of marching about the hut. One brave crew member from the AMC nailed the boots to the crew room wall, where they'll stay forever.

THE HIKE

AMMONUSIC RAVINE TRAIL TO LAKES OF THE CLOUDS TO HUT/MT. WASHINGTON SUMMIT 👻👻👻👻

The Trailhead to the Ammonusic Ravine Trail begins from the parking lot at Base Road. Base Road can be accessed from Rte. 302 in Crawford Notch. When combined with the upper section of the Crawford Path, it is the shortest route to Mt. Washington from the west. The trail follows the headwaters of the Ammonoosuc River and there are beautiful views along the way, especially toward the upper section where deep gorges account for outstanding views. From the parking lot, the trail follows a path through a wooded section. At .3 miles, the trail crosses Franklin Brook, and skirts Base Station area. It joins the old route of the trail at 1.0 mile. The main trail bears right along the river. The grade is moderate, but can be slippery. Take extra caution on wet rocks. The trail ascends gradually, and then crosses Monroe Brook at 1.7 miles. At 2.1 miles it crosses the outlet of Gem Pool. At 2.3 miles the trail becomes rough and steep. A fine viewpoint at the foot of the gorge can be seen from here.

The trail continues steeply and crosses the main brook at 2.5 on ledges. At 3.0 miles, the trail moderates. The trail follows a line of cairns up a series of rock slabs then passes through a patchy area of scrub. At 3.1 miles the trail reaches the Crawford Path at the south side of the Lakes of the Clouds Hut. Approximate time is 3 hours.

FROM THE LAKES OF THE CLOUDS HUT TO MT. WASHINGTON VIA CRAWFORD PATH 👻👻👻👻

After visiting the AMC Lakes of the Clouds Hut, the summit of Mt. Washington (6288') can be reached via the Crawford Path. From the hut, the Crawford Path crosses an outlet of one of the lakes then passes between them. The trail ascends at moderate grades to the North West side of the ridge. Take caution to stay on the Crawford Path, as many other trails intersect at various junctions.

The Crawford path runs north up the cone of Mt. Washington in a steep climb. Washington summit is reached in 1.5 miles.

From Lakes of the Clouds Hut (5012') and junction with Crawford Path:

To Westside Trail junction:	.9 mile
To junction of Gulfside Trail:	1.3 miles
To Mt. Washington summit:	1.5 miles
Approximate time:	Additional 1–2 hours.

Lost Souls and Angels

The Gulf is a vast bowl of thick wilderness between Mt. Washington, Jefferson and Adams, and it is known for its wild weather. There are stories of people who have just simply disappeared off Mt. Washington's summit. In 1890, a musician named Ewald Weiss left the summit house on Mt. Washington and was never seen alive again. The same thing happened in 1912 when another young man vanished. John Keenan was only eighteen years old. He was hired as a surveyor and also disappeared. The remains of both men have never been found.

There are many stories that speak of "The Presence." It may be a force that embodies the anguished souls who have perished on the mountain. Many believe the Great Gulf is haunted.

The Presence appears as an entity and acts as a force—the force of a wind blast so powerful it feels as if you've been struck by an object. But then again, this is Mt. Washington, where the most powerful and deadliest winds in the world have been recorded.

Some hikers have reported a kindlier presence on the mountain. They are referred to as "Trail Angels," and many lost hikers have seen them throughout the Presidential Range and even in the Pemigewasset Wilderness Area. One man was

The mysterious winter hiker seemed to have vanished.

hiking in Tuckerman's Ravine one winter and found he had taken the wrong trail through the bowl of Tuckerman's. He was trying to get over the Lions Head where the path was. He was about to turn around when he saw a figure of a man just ahead of him. The man was dressed in dark woolen clothes and wore a strange hat.

He gestured to the lost hiker the correct way to go, leading him back to the path. Later, as the lost hiker found the correct winter path to the summit, he saw the man again and wanted to thank him. The man told him to be very careful going down. On the descent, the hiker looked for the man to follow him back down. The mysterious winter hiker seemed to have vanished.

Other hikers have had similar experiences of a mysterious hiker who appears ahead of them and encourages them to continue in spite of their exhaustion, or who helps them find their way back to the trail. It is inexplicable and has happened to many who have lost their way on the trail. The hiker snapped a picture of his "guide." The photo depicts a dark figure running through the deep snow. He says he will never forget the experience. "It's as if this guide was meant to be there at the very place and time when I needed the help," he said. "When I looked back up, he was gone." Whether they are angels or simply "helpful guides" that appear when needed, there is no doubting that the trail and paths in the White Mountains are filled with mystery and spiritual energy.

You can make your reservation to stay at any one of the AMC huts. Carter Hut is open year round. Lakes of the Clouds is only open for the summer season. Sleeping over at the huts is an experience like no other, but bring an extra flashlight and keep it with you. You never know who could be creeping around your bunk at night!

The AMC website is www.outdoors.org. For Hut reservations contact Pinkham Notch Visitor Center at 603-466-2727.

AMC Lakes of the Clouds Hut via Ammonoosuc Ravine Trail: A challenging 3.1 mile hike from parking area at Base Rd. WMNF parking fees apply at trailhead parking.

Time:	Allow 3 hours to hut. Allow 4–5 hours for a continuation of hike to Mt. Washington summit. A difficult and strenuous climb, not recommended for young children.
What to look for:	Gorges, cascades, and Gem Pool. At the Lakes of the Clouds hut, look for Ben Campbell's boots.

Things to consider: Is there a Presence lurking
                               about the AMC hut at 5,012'?
                               Have an AMC Crew member
                               tell you a story!

Carter Notch Hut via Nineteen Mile Brook Trail: A moderate-challenging 3.8 miles.

Time: Allow 3 hours to hut. Add
                               additional one hour or more
                               to Carter Dome summit, via
                               Carter-Moriah Trail, to Carter
                               Dome at 4,832'. A strenuous and
                               steep 1.2 miles from Nineteen
                               Mile Brook Trail. Parking fee at
                               Nineteen-Mile Brook Trail parking
                               terminus Rte. 16.

What to look for: The ghost of Red Mac and the
                               tramping of his snowy boots on
                               the hut roof. Look for Red Mac's
                               lantern in the thick woods of
                               Carter Notch!

For more information
Contact AMC: (603) 466-2727
                               www.outdoors.org

Mt. Washington Weather
Observatory: www.mountwashington.org

Bayle Mountain
Ossipee Mountains Tract
Ossipee, NH

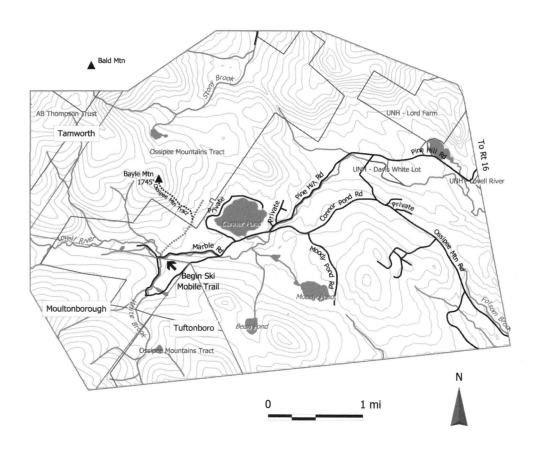

Bald Mtn

AB Thompson Trust

Stony Brook

UNH – Lord Farm

Tamworth

Ossipee Mountains Tract

Pine Hill Rd

To Rt 16

Bayle Mtn
1745'

Ossipee Mtn Tract

UNH – Davis White Lot

Private

Pine Hill Rd

UNH – Lovell River

Private

Connor Pond Rd

Private

Connor Pond

Lovell River

Marble Rd

Moody Pond Rd

Ossipee Mtn Rd

Begin Ski
Mobile Trail

Moody Pond

Folsom Brook

Moultonborough

White Brook

Tuftonboro

Bean Pond

Ossipee Mountains Tract

0   1 mi

N

8 Sasquatch of Ossipee

Don't be sad
Don't be Gloomy
Pitch your tent
At Gitchee Goumee!

The Ossipee Mountain Range is a complex and magnificent geological wonder. These low lying mountains form a rare, near-perfect ring dike. The dike formation are the remains of a volcanic chamber formed 120 million years ago that ran four miles deep underneath the earth's surface. As magma flowed upward over fractured granite, a wall-like ring dike was created. The dike is internationally recognized and attracts geologists and prospectors alike. The mixed composition of volcanic rock and coarse grained granite is somewhat of an anomaly.

Through the 1960s and '70s, hordes of children enjoyed Camp Gitchee Goumee in West Ossipee. Their stays included swimming in the river, midnight raids, and marshmallow roasts. For many of those children, the ghost stories are what they remember most. While the mosquitoes buzzed and the camp counselors slept unknowingly, the kids relayed the stories they heard each and every year as they munched on forbidden candy well into night. The scariest and most terrifying was the one about the monster that lived in the Ossipee Mountains, referred to as the monster of Gitchee Goumee. This beast was over seven-feet tall and covered in gray hair with black piercing eyes. It ate children, mostly the unlucky ones who wandered away from the camp grounds or dared to hike off into the trail-less wilderness of the Ossipee Mountain Range.

Of course the Monster of Gitchee Goumee was only a concoction of children's overactive imagination. Or, could the monster be real?

At the turn of the century, an unusual sighting of a monster or Sasquatch was rumored to have occurred in West Ossipee. On Conner Pond, a group of friends and family gathered outside a cabin in early spring as the ice was melting on the pond. A small dog wandered onto the ice and fell in. Suddenly, out of the woods a large, hairy man-Beast appeared. He walked onto the ice and rescued the dog to the shock and amazement of everyone present. As mysteriously as the creature emerged, he disappeared back into the woods again.

Tales of a Sasquatch in the mountains of the Ossipee Range have been around for years. In Moultonborough, growling and inhuman howling has been reported by locals and tourists camping in the wild. Just north of Ossipee, near Thornton, large unusual footprints were spotted in the snow. Other tracks were recorded and made into casts in the area of Waterville Valley. Though some hair samples were collected at these sites, the evidence was inconclusive. What no one can explain, however, is how the prints were made, and more importantly, who made them. Over the years, the earth shattering howling, yowling and screams are reported from as far south as Loudon. Skeptics argue that these cries and howls are simply owls or coyote. Try telling that to Peter Samualson.

Suddenly, out of the woods, a large, hairy man-beast appeared.

One of the most intriguing stories to come out of the Ossipee Mountains concerns the strange encounter that prospector and hiker Peter Samualson experienced with his girlfriend and dog "Kat" in 1979 that has baffled critics and non-believers. An antiques dealer from Maine, Samualson has hiked and prospected over these mountains for many years. At sixty-eight, his days of bushwhacking mountains in search of quartz are mostly over. But he will never forget the wild encounter he and his friend Holly experienced on a summer day near Bald Mountain.

It is fair to describe the ledges and summits of many of the mountains in this vast ring dike as remote, distant, unreachable and isolated. Though hunters have created game trails over the years, most of these mountains can only be reached with a good compass and a reliable GPS system. Samualson was bushwhacking up the northern side of Bald Mountain in search of topaz crystals. He and Holly had packs loaded with supplies: cameras, water, and food. As they reached the ledges looking out to Conner Pond, Samualson caught sight of something unusual just one hundred yards ahead.

Kat began growling, and the fur on his back rose in terror. Samualson saw a granite dwelling with an entrance and a thatched roof. There, inside the structure, was a giant hairy man over seven feet tall. The hair on his towering body was grayish in color, tangled and unkempt. Peter never saw the face of the creature, only the backside. For an instant he and Holly froze. Then they heard the creature howl "the most ungodly, inhuman sound I have ever heard in my life," says Samualson. "It is something I can never forget." Immediately they fled, rushing down the mountain in a panic, going as fast as their feet could take them. They did not look back. Samualson tried returning to the site with a group of other curiosity seekers, but he was unable to locate the exact spot where he had been earlier. He has been up to Bald Mountain again and again since that time, but has not found anything that even suggested that a den had been created there. To this day, Samualson stands by his story. "I know what I saw that day and I will never forget it."

Has the Sasquatch made other appearances in New Hampshire? You better believe it. In northern Coos County, residents refer to these hominids as Wood Devils, close cousins to Sasquatch or Bigfoot. Sightings of the slender, hairy Wood Devils have been recorded in the Berlin and Salisbury areas. Hunters and woodsmen have known about them for years. They appear deep in the woods and move very quickly!

THE HIKES

BALD MT. HIKE (ELEV. 2,123')

You can visit Bald Mountain in Ossipee and have a look for yourself, but bring a GPS system and compass, and don't forget your sense of direction. Bushwhacking through this territory is potentially dangerous if you should become lost. Most areas are thick with overgrowth, and deep cavernous ledges are abound throughout the northern mountains. Footing is rough. There are no trails beyond the trail that lead to Bayle Mountain. This trail leaves from a popular ski-mobile corridor that runs through the area. Caverns and boulder fields are prominent. Perhaps these caves hide a secret link to an underground world. Maybe the answer to this puzzling mystery lies miles below the earth's surface in the ancient chambers of Ossipee's rugged terrain. But be very careful, or the monster of Gitchee Goumee just might getcha!

WHERE IS THIS PLACE?

Where was Sasquatch seen?

Peter Samuelson and his hiking partner spotted the Sasquatch on the ledges of Bald Mt. in Tamworth, a remote mountain in the Ossipee Mountain Range. Peter began his hike from Gilman Valley Road in Tamworth, making his way down the old gravel road then bushwhacking to the ledges of Bald Mt. without use of a compass or GPS tracking device. He was familiar with the rough territory and was physically fit and well prepared.

There are a number of hikes in the Ossipee Mountains. Bayle Mt. is located 1.5 miles south of Bald Mt. in the town of Ossipee and is easily accessible. Fantastic views of the Ossipee Mountains await from the open summit on Bayle Mt. The trail is well marked with red blazes and passes through a fantastic boulder field half way to the peak. From the top of Bayle you can gaze upon one of the greatest geologic wonders of the world. Millions of years ago these mountains were part of a chain of volcanoes that stood 40,000 feet! Today what remains is a perfectly circular ring dike, one of only 28 in the world.

HIKE TO BAYLE MT. (ELEV. 1,709') 　　👻👻

Follow the wide, grassy ski mobile trail from the gated entrance, at Marble Rd. in Ossipee. The trail has good footing and there are signs along the way. Continue for .7 miles looking to the left hand side of the trail for the cairn marking the trail head to Bayle Mt. (not entirely obvious). The cairn, on the left, is also marked by a nearby tree with blazes. The trail to the summit of Bayle Mt. is well blazed and steep in some parts. The rocky ledges of the open summit is reached in an easy .5 miles. The peak has a hiker's registry, and there is usually an American flag flown from the peak. To the north, just beyond two wooded knolls, rises Bald Mt., about 1.5 miles from Bayle. You can end your hike here, on the gorgeous summit of Bayle Mt.

Bayle Mountain, via ski-mobile corridor, to unnamed trail to Bayle summit:

1.2 mile hike to the beautiful panoramic summit.

Time:	Allow 2–3 hours for round trip hike.
Parking:	Get permission if parking on private property. Park at ski mobile gate at Marble Rd.
What to look for:	Boulder fields, fantastic views from the summit.
What to consider:	Is there a Sasquatch living in the remote hills and mountains of the Ossipees?

WHERE IS THIS PLACE?

Rte. 16 traveling north, take a left onto Pine Hill Road, located across from Pizza Barn. Follow Pine Hill Road for 3.4 miles. At the end of Pine Hill Road take a right to Conner Pond Road. Follow Conner Pond Road for .5 miles to the junction of Marble and Bean Mountain Road, bear right onto Marble Road, and go .6 miles to a brook crossing. Park near the gated entrance to the ski-mobile trail on the right. The main artery of the ski-mobile trail can be picked up from here.

Total mileage from Marble Road to Bayle Mt. summit: 1.2 miles. 2.4 miles round trip.

(Bayle Mountain is protected conservation land under the Ossipee Mountain Tract. Trails here are maintained under the New Hampshire Department of Resource and Economic Development. The land is privately owned by Chocorua Forest Lands, LLC.)

9 Chief Chocorua and a Legendary Mountain Curse

Chief Chocorua, a Pigwacket widower, was a study in dichotomy. A shaman with dark sad eyes, he was often a friend to the early settlers of a township in the Swift River Valley. He may have been a great grandson of the great sachem Passaconoway. In the early 1700s, the majority of Abenaki fled for safer ground while the British armies waged war upon their people. Chocorua was different. As the white colonists moved north, encroaching upon his once pristine territory, Chocorua welcomed his neighbors, all the while keeping himself at a safe distance. His wisdom and knowledge were invaluable to the settlers and yet he kept them at bay. In this way, he kept the upper hand.

The new settlers consisted of Scotsmen and Englishmen. They had come to occupy these territories and stake a claim to freedom, but in so doing they paid the price of security. Cornelius Campbell and his wife and children settled in this remote and rugged wilderness valley, and soon befriended the Pigwacket chief, in spite of his reluctance to trust the foreigners. Between the Scotsman and the lone chief, another relationship blossomed: the friendship of Campbell's young son and Chocorua's ten-year-old boy. In the sparsely settled community, the two boys played tirelessly. Chocorua perhaps saw his own son benefiting from the friendship, particularly since Mrs. Campbell watched over the boy and seemed to have a special place in her heart for him. Having lost his mother early on, Chocorua's son was drawn to Mrs. Campbell's care, and to the tasty desserts she baked.

Chocorua was often gone for days, either negotiating with the St. Francis Indians to the north, or seeking peace and solitude among the steep jagged cliffs in the mountains. He was drawn to one single domed mountain in the valley. The settlers in town knew it as "Chocorua's peak."

Champney Falls Loop Trail & Piper Trail

Mt Chocura Scenic Area - Albany, NH

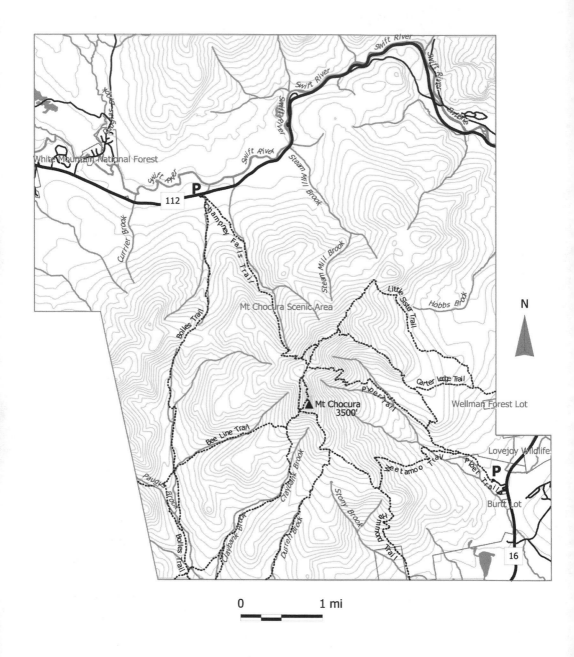

0   1 mi

Over time Campbell and the Chief bonded in a unique friendship. Campbell looked to the chief to offer help and suggestions to ease the incredible hardship of pioneer life. Rocky soil made it difficult to grow crops. Indian raids were common, and wild animals ravaged their livestock. Children grew weak with unknown illnesses, and daily life was a struggle against the odds. Chocorua educated these early pioneers about the medicinal benefits of herbs and other cures. He offered techniques to help the farmers who were unfamiliar with the land.

Though they were grateful, there was something about the chief that made many settlers uneasy. Chocorua's brooding temperament was intimidating, and for the most part, the settlers kept a safe distance.

One morning Chocorua announced he would be leaving for a trip. His attendance was required at an important mission involving the great leaders along the St. Francis. In an understood agreement between the men, the Campbell's would look after Chocorua's son while he was gone. They were happy to take care of the boy, but soon after Chocorua left for the trip something went horribly wrong.

Campbell was experiencing a problem on his property with foxes. The intruders would sneak into the farm and steal chickens and eggs. Campbell made every attempt to keep the animals off his property. He had laid traps for the sly beasts, but the foxes were too clever. Even the two boys made a game of trying to catch the animals but it was no use. Campbell thought of a plan to rid his farm of the vagrants once and for all: he would poison them. He fetched a bottle of lethal poison and began at once to saturate bait with the sticky stuff. The curious smell of the poison intrigued Chocorua's young son. Thinking it was sweet molasses from Mrs. Campbell's cupboard, the boy drank the deadly concoction. Immediately, he became violently ill. For an entire night the child vomited and clutched his sides in pain and anguish. The Campbells did everything they could to comfort him, but he did not recover. By morning, his limp body lay dead in the eerie silence of the Campbell home. Cornelius dug a grave by a great boulder and they laid the little boy to rest. How would they tell their friend that his one and only son had perished under their care?

The Campbells did everything they could to comfort him, but he did not recover.

Chocorua returned from his trip and the husband and wife quietly approached him with the terrible news. The chief was beyond consolation and could not accept that his son's death was an accident. He left the Campbell's cabin and retreated for the rugged mountain ledges. His cries of torture cut through the night, and for days it seemed Chocorua would not ever recover from the loss. Cornelius waited at the cabin for the chief to return. They would help him through his loss. But the chief remained at the mountain top in his grief stricken state, in complete isolation. But Caroline Campbell was optimistic, and told her husband not to worry, he would eventually come around. He just needed time. Maybe his wife was right, and the chief just needed some privacy on his secluded mountain. But Campbell still felt a nagging sense of doubt.

One day he left his family at the cabin and went into town to run some errands. Upon returning home, he noticed that the farm was quiet. The children were not out playing, and his wife was not hanging the clothing to dry. The silence was disturbing. Inside the silent cabin, Cornelius made a gruesome discovery. His wife and children lay in heaps, their flesh hacked to shreds and their bones crushed. Blood splattered the walls and ceilings. His entire family had been butchered. A fierce rage festered within Cornelius's soul. Only one man could possibly be responsible for the cold-blooded murders, he decided: Chocorua!

Gathering strength, he went to each of the bodies of his wife and children, vowing revenge. Before leaving the cabin, he loaded his rifle with flint and slung it over his back. Neighbors soon learned of the tragedy as Campbell made his way to the mountain where he knew he would find the chief. A group of excited Englishmen followed suit, packing their rifles and hurrying to the mountain's edge. Infuriated, the hunt for Chocorua was on! They marched through swamp and thick spruce forest and up the steep granite ledges of the magnificent cone to the very summit. They found Chocorua, just as Campbell expected, sitting at a boulder on the very peak of the mountain, overlooking the

THE CHOCORUA LEGEND

In several versions, the legend's sequence relates the mysterious death of Chocorua's son while in the care of a settler named Campbell. Suspicious of the cause, the Pequawket chieftain took revenge on the settler's family. Then, in retaliation, Campbell killed Chocorua on the peak of the mountain now bearing the Indian's name.

small village 3,400 feet below him. At last Cornelius confronted the murderous chief, and ordered him to jump to his death. Indignantly, Chocorua refused by telling him, "the Great Spirit gave life to Chocorua, and he will not throw it away at the command of the white man."

Outraged, Campbell shouted, "Then hear your Great Spirit speak in the white man's thunder!" Campbell pressed his rifle against Chocorua's side to fire. Chocorua's figure remained perfectly still as the gun took aim, but his arms rose up as if he would take flight. In a booming voice, echoing throughout the valley, Chocorua beckoned the great spirits and the powerful forces from beyond. He cried, "A curse upon ye, white men! Chocorua had a son and ye killed him! Lightning *A curse upon ye,* blast your crops! Wind and fire destroy your *white men!* dwellings! Evil One breath death on your cattle. Wolves will fatten upon your bones. Chocorua goes to the Great Spirit, but his curse stays with the white man!"

Gun powder exploded and rattled the earth. Chocorua rose from the boulder and thrust himself off the cliff to the rocky abyss below.

A dreadful silence passed over the mountain top and Campbell stopped to collect his thoughts before returning back down the path. Overcome with a moral obligation, he later returned to search for the mangled body on the ledges. He carried the body into the forest and buried it along the trail. Then Cornelius returned home to deal with the unthinkable burden of burying his wife and children.

Soon after, a mysterious plague infected the cattle of Burton and other surrounding villages. The cattle were dying off in remarkable numbers. The town's people became spooked and left Burton in fear of the dreaded Indian's curse. Amidst raids by bears, wolves, and savage Indians, the residents of the small community were convinced: Chocorua's curse had come to be. The villagers even had their town's name changed to Albany, but to no avail. Instead, a wailing chorus can be still be heard carrying through the crevices of Mt. Chocorua's isolated peak. It is the cry of angered spirits; a deafening chorus for the unforgiven.

Two years after Chocorua's death, Cornelius's body was discovered long after he had died. He had never fully recovered from the traumatic loss of his family. He became a hermit and built a secluded home in the forest. His decaying corpse was removed and buried deep in the woods. The graves of Chocorua, Campbell, and the Campbell family are hidden deep in the forest of the Sandwich Wilderness. Their graves are as much a mystery as Chocorua's legend. You can climb to Cow Rock, where Chocorua took his fatal plunge. And you can take a dip in the beautiful lake that bears his name. But whatever you do, don't break the silence of these sacred waters. It will anger the Great Spirits and invoke the ancient curse once more!

WHERE IS THIS PLACE?

Take Rte. 16 to Chocorua Village, .6 miles south of the junction of Rte. 112 (Kancamagus Highway). The trailhead begins at the parking area located behind Davies General Store in Albany.

PIPER TRAIL—A CHALLENGING HIKE TO CHOCORUA'S SUMMIT

The Piper Trail enters a wooded area at the edge of the parking lot and swings right, crossing a stream. It then joins an old woods road, which is an old route of the trail. The Nickerson Ledge Trail diverges to the right at 1.2 miles. The trail crosses the Chocorua River at 1.8 miles, and then the trail begins to climb moderately. At 2.8 miles a spur path diverges left to Camp Penacook, where a sign is visible. At 3.6 miles the Champney Falls Trail enters from the right, and the West Side Trail enters from the right in another .2 miles. The Piper Trail continues over scenic open ledges to a junction with the Brook Trail then climbs steeply to the summit at 4.3 miles.

NICKERSON LEDGE—A MODERATE HIKE ON MT. CHOCORUA

For a moderate hike with equally impressive views, a hike from the Piper trail to Nickerson Ledge Trail to Nickerson Ledge is less challenging, but still scenic. This trail leaves the Piper Trail at 1.2 miles. It reaches Nickerson ledge at .2 miles from the junction with the Piper Trail, making this an easier hike for younger children.

CHAMPNEY FALLS TRAIL TO
MT. CHOCORUA, ALBANY

Here is a fantastic hike to picturesque and cursed Mt. Chocorua summit up the Champney Falls Trail off Rte. 112, Kancamagus Highway. An alternate moderate hike to Champney and Pitcher Falls, round trip 3.2 miles, can also be accessed from the Champney Falls Trail. The strenuous hike to Mt. Chocorua's rocky cone, with outstanding 360 degree views all around is a difficult 7.6 miles round trip via the Champney Falls Trail-Piper Trail. Though the rewards are fantastic, be prepared to do some very rough climbing if you should choose to complete the hike all the way to Chocorua's summit at (3500').

CHAMPNEY FALLS TRAIL LOOP

This popular trail leaves from Kancamagus Highway, 11.5 miles from junction with Rte. 16 in Conway. The trail has moderate grades. Park at the trailhead parking off Rte. 112. The trail begins here and soon crosses Twin Brook. At .1 mile the Bolles Trail diverges to the right. The trail continues with easy grades along an old logging road to Champney Brook. At 1.4 miles it reaches the loop path to the left, which leads to scenic Pitcher Falls and Champney Falls. Use caution along the ledges here which can be slippery and dangerous. The loop trail rejoins the main trail, passing the scenic falls area in .4 miles.

Round trip mileage to the Champney Falls Loop hike and returning to the parking area is 3.2 miles.

To continue to the summit of Mt. Chocorua from the Champney Falls loop, continue along the Champney Falls Trail. At 2.4 miles there is a good view out to the north and begins an ascent with several switchbacks. At 3.0 miles the Middle Sister cutoff diverges left. The trail then reaches what looks like a ledge for a spur path to an outlook on the right. At 3.2 the trail ends at a junction with the Piper Trail.

From this point take the Piper Trail which reaches the summit of Mt. Chocorua in .6 miles. In .2 miles the West Side trail enters on the right. The Piper trail continues along over ledges with fine open views. The main trail has another junction with the Brook

Trail, and then continues over steep ledges to the rocky summit. The cubicle rock known as "The Cow" doesn't really resemble a cow at all. It is here, that as legend goes, Chocorua threw himself into the abyss.

Hike estimation:	Chocorua summit via Champney Falls Trail/Piper Trail: 3.8 miles
Time:	Allow Three hours or more. Strenuous and challenging.
Champney Falls loop Trail to Champney and Pitcher Falls:	Approximately 2.1 miles moderate hike to scenic falls and return to parking terminus at Rte. 112.
Parking:	WMNF parking fee area.
What to look for:	Cow Rock, the suicidal leaping point of the famous chief on the summit of the mountain. Also, scenic waterfalls and 360 degree panoramic views of Mt. Washington Valley from Chocorua's cone.
What to consider:	Are the woods haunted or cursed by Chief Chocorua's?
For more information Contact:	AMC: (603)466-2727 www.mtwashingtonvalley. org 1- (877) -948-6867

WHERE IS THIS PLACE?

The Champney Falls trailhead is located on Rte. 112, Kancamagus Highway 11.5 miles from the junction at Rte. 16 in Conway.

10 The Cursed Rangers — Mt. Adams

I n the years from 1756 to 1763, the Rangers were a hardcore army of fierce mountain men from northern New England. Under British rule, these rag-tag men in their green uniforms battled their enemies: the French and Abenaki Indians. Surprise Indian raids upon colonial villages were common. The bold Natives scalped the white settlers, kidnapped women and children, and brought mayhem, disorder, and fear to the early settlers of New Hampshire and Vermont. Though the Indians moved north along the Hudson River for their own protection, the raids continued.

Major Robert Rogers from Portsmouth was appointed by the Royal Crown Army to lead the Rangers to victory over the enemy. Rogers recruited a select group of rugged reliable men who knew the mountainous terrain of the Northwest Passage. In 1759, Rogers and his men were given orders to raid an Indian village along the St. Francis River near Quebec. The village was Odinak, a community of three hundred Indians and their Jesuit missionaries. The invasion was meant to disgrace the enemy and put an end once and for all to the Indian raids on the colonists. What followed this murderous mission is a legend of massacre, madness, curses, and cannibalism, and to this day, hidden treasures from their rampages are purported to lay buried in the White Mountains. But these sacred artifacts may be better left undiscovered.

Trouble with Roger's mission began even before the Rangers started out.

In 1754 the American Colonies were in the French and Indian War. The conflict over trade and land between England's King George II and France's King Louis XV directly involved the new settlers. For seven years the British army, strengthened by the colonists, battled the French and native Indians, their pillaging armies, and violent death raids. The British found that its own corps of soldiers were not effectively trained to battle in the harsh wilderness. The Crown appointed a settler from southern New

Snyder Brook Scenic Area - Appalachia Trailhead
Mt. Adams - Randolph, NH

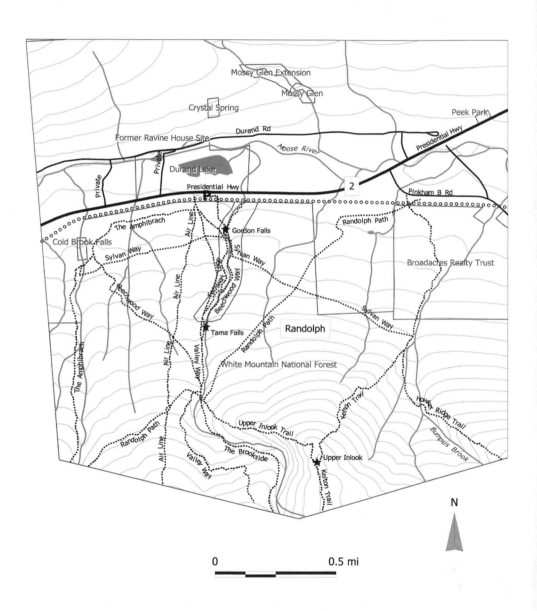

0   0.5 mi

N

Hampshire, Robert Rogers, as major. He created his own army of soldiers called Rogers Rangers. These hardened men were familiar with the territory along the Hudson River to Quebec. Their brutality was well known. They were idolized as heroes by the early settlers who lived in perpetual fear of raids. Their style of attack would be comparable to guerrilla warfare. The Rangers and the demanding Major Rogers left for the area of St. Francis in September of 1759 from Fort Crown Point at Lake Champlain. Uniformed and packing their crude instruments of destruction, the two hundred Rangers believed this was to be their most important and deadly mission.

The men were to cross the lake to Missiquoi Bay, but a series of terrible setbacks seemed to indicate bad omens. First, a keg of gun powder exploded and sixty men were injured and had to turn back. Then, after reaching the bay, they learned that their boats and provisions were stolen by the French and Indians. Their enemies were on their trail! For twenty days the army of Rangers trod through thickets of mud, swamp, and forest over a hundred miles. Convinced that the Indians were right behind them, they dared not sleep or stop for rest. Rogers should have heeded the omens as a bad sign, but instead he stubbornly pressed his troops on. After the theft of their boats and supplies, Rogers planned for an alternate route on their return. The battle hadn't even begun and already their situation was bleak. The major sent a scout to make sure provisions would be ready upon their arrival at a fort on the upper Connecticut River. When they finally reached the Odinak Village, the men were hungry and overcome with paranoia and sleep deprivation—a dangerous combination.

They overtook the sleeping village of St. Francis at daybreak. Their attack was bloodthirsty. The Rangers slipped into wigwams and quietly sliced the necks of sleeping villagers. When the others awoke, chaos prevailed as many screamed in terror trying to escape. The Rangers, prepared for a mass exodus, had already punched holes in their canoes. In an adrenaline charged frenzy, the killing raged on without pity. Even children were butchered in the massacre. Between drowning, stabbing, and musket balls, Indians fell to their deaths in huge numbers.

Then in full view, the Rangers caught sight of a stockade fence decorated with the ornaments of scalps from white prisoners. Their rage intensified. A small group of Indians managed to flee the bloodshed and hide in the sanctuary of the Jesuit church, but Ranger Benjamin Bradley and his men found them. The Jesuit priest begged for mercy, pleading to the killers, "This is the house of God!" Surrounded by glowing candles and glimmering artifacts of the church, the Rangers laughed at their victims, and did not give mercy. Instead, they shot the priest point blank, and slaughtered the trembling refuges like animals in a murderous blood bath.

A small group of Indians managed to flee the bloodshed and hide in the sanctuary of the Jesuit church, but Ranger Benjamin Bradley and his men found them.

But they didn't stop there. The rampaging men looted the church and stole the gold candlesticks, coins, and artifacts, before setting the building on fire. Among the stolen items was a ten-pound silver statue of the Virgin Mary. As the church burned, the bells tolled and crashed in the fire. Suddenly, a deep and disturbing voice rose from the conflagration amidst the heap of burning corpses. A curse was laid upon these murderous monsters and a voice spoke, "The Great Spirit will scatter darkness in the path of the accursed pale-faces. Hunger and death strikes their trail. Manitou is angry when the dead speak and the dead have spoken!"

The small band of Rangers hurriedly left the blazing church with their stolen treasures. By then, the entire army of Rangers fled fearing an inevitable attack. Brady's group hid the sacred valuables in their knapsacks and headed at once to the River. The Rangers made it as far as Lake Memphramagog, on what is now the Canadian/Vermont border. Rogers, sensing retaliation, broke the large group of 130 men into smaller groups, believing that smaller groups would better deter the enemy. He ordered the bands to meet once again along the river where supplies would be waiting for them. The disbanded groups now set about fighting for their own individual survival. One party of Rangers was attacked and killed by Indians.

The men were all in a state of turmoil fueled by panic, hunger, and fatigue. They were near starvation and weak from the grueling mission, but breaking for rest and food threatened their safety. They could not, and did not, let up. When Major Rogers's group finally reached the Connecticut River, there was nothing there—

the fort was in ruins. Just as the curse had stated, death and hunger marked their trail.

Bradley's group, carrying the weight of the stolen treasure, proceeded south but was struck by a blinding snowstorm. Their confusion was made worse as they became lost in the wilderness. Their plans changed and the remaining group, now down to four, decided to walk all the way to Concord, New Hampshire. They removed the sacred treasures from their packs and buried them, hid them in caves, or flung them into the deep woods. One by one they died of hunger and exhaustion.

The remaining Rangers crossed the Connecticut River and sought out a guide to take them through the Great Pass of Crawford Notch. They met an Indian who agreed to lead them to the Great Pass, but no farther. The men hid more of the treasure near what is today Littleton. The guide grew anxious of the Great Spirits of Agiochook, or Mt. Washington, whose anger was fearsome, and abandoned the men. But before leaving, he drew them a crude map on birch bark with a rattlesnake fang. By accident, he scratched one of the Rangers with the poisonous tip. The poison drove the Ranger to madness and he killed himself. The three Rangers left began to believe that they truly were cursed. The last of the artifacts they carried was the statue of the Virgin Mary. The men decided the statue must be the source of their curse, and buried it with their comrade somewhere east of Littleton and north of the Great Pass.

Two more Rangers met their deaths due to starvation and madness. Only one, Sergeant Parsons, made it to the Pass, and was found crawling on his hands and knees with knives and a heavy pack in his possession. Inside the pack was a gruesome discovery: the severed head of one of his companions. Parsons had been eating the flesh of the dead to stay alive.

As the years passed, much of the Rangers treasure has been recovered. In 1816 the gold candlesticks were found in Vermont. A Canadian woman found silver plates on her farm property in 1998. Along the Rangers' unfortunate route others have found coins, buttons, and human bones. The silver Madonna, however, has not been discovered. Plenty of treasure hunters have searched the valley for her, but she remains hidden in some thicket or overgrowth, or even in the Israel River.

Incarnations of Bradley and the ghoulish souls of the priest killers have been seen in the northern Mt. Washington Valley, along the slopes of Mt. Adams. It is said that the Indian guide led the men upstream to the foot of this great ravine near the Israel River before he vanished. A hunter once camped at this very spot and had a remarkable vision. He saw a great stone church with Indians inside, praying on their knees. But then the granite doors closed locking 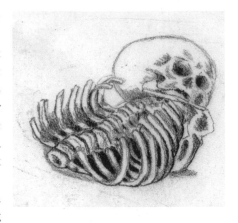 nine souls outside. These nine followed a floating statue, each one suffering from starvation and wailing in agony.

Should you find the silver statue on your hiking adventure, you may be wise to leave her be. Manitou's curse would scatter darkness in your path and hunger and death upon your trail. Worst of all, you might end up eating your friends for lunch! But if you find the Madonna, you'd be set for life. The statue is worth millions.

Scenic Hikes on Mt. Adams

Mt. Adams has always been regarded as a place of deep mystery and spiritual energy. Some believe that the Great Gulf is also haunted! In Myths and Legends of our own Lands, Charles Skinner described visions on Mt. Adams that were disturbing and frightening. Skinner documented that spirits of the famished group of Rangers were "wont for many winters to cry in the woods." The forms were said to march in silence following a floating silver image that spread a pair of wings and soared above.

A hike to the summit of Mt. Adams is extremely strenuous and has a high degree of difficulty. Much of the upper section of trails are above tree line making for weather exposed conditions. Hiking in any area of the White Mountains above tree line can be treacherous in bad weather conditions.

Below is a variety of moderate loop hikes on Mt. Adams each offering a scenic route through gorgeous waterfalls.

To reach the Appalachia parking area, where the hikes below are accessed, take Rte. 2 into Randolph. The trailhead is well marked and 1 mile west of Pinkham Road.

FALLSWAY/BROOKBANK LOOP
TO TAMA FALLS. SNYDER BROOK
SCENIC AREA

Begin at the Appalachia parking area along Rte. 2 in Randolph. Take the Fallsway at the far left of the parking lot. (Airline Trail is to the far right). Hike along the Fallsway to Gordon Fall at .15 miles. Continue past the junction of Sylvan Way to junction with Valley Way and Tama Falls, .6 miles. Descend via Brook bank Trail to junction of Sylvan Way at .5 miles. Hike on Sylvan way for just .01 mile back to the Fallsway returning to Appalachia. Total is 1.5 miles, taking approximately 1 hour.

VIEWPOINT AT DOME ROCK AND
UPPER INLOOK

The Dome Rock Loop begins at the Appalachia Parking area. Hike on the Airline Trail for .3 miles to Valley Way, then to Maple Walk. Follow Maple Walk to Sylvan Way to junction of Howker Ridge Trail. Follow Howker Ridge Trail .07 miles to Kelton Trail. Follow Kelton Trail .9 miles to Upper Inlook. Hike .7 miles on Inlook Trail to junction with The Brookside and Randolph Path. Dome rock is located on the descent along the Inlook Trail and affords incredible views. Descend The Brookside to Valley Way to Fallsway, or Maple Walk, and then back to Appalachia Parking area. Total is 4.0. Allow 3 to 4 hours.

Nancy Brook Scenic Area - Nancy Pond Trail

Harts Location, NH

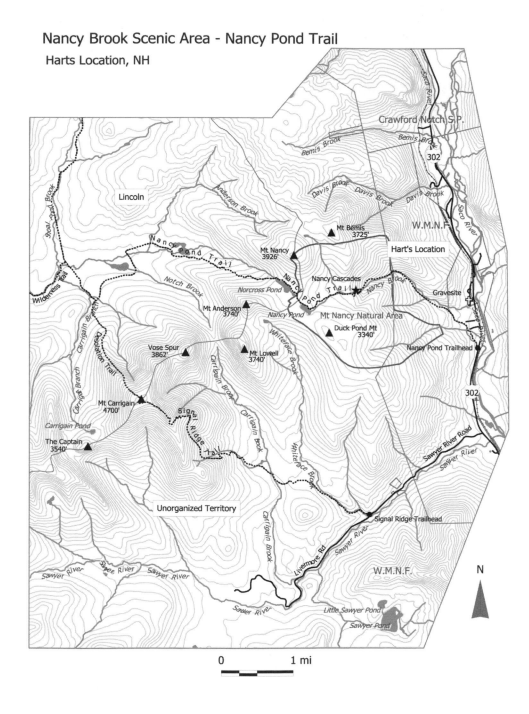

11 The Lost Love and Last Journey of Nancy Barton

Nancy Barton worked as a servant girl under Colonel Joseph Whipple in 1778. It was on his farm in Jefferson that she met a young man named Jim, a farmhand, with whom she fell in love when she was sixteen. Nancy was known as a hard working, honest young lady. These qualities, she believed, she had also found in Jim. Together, they planned for a future wedding in Portsmouth. Jim would soon be heading there and he promised to take her along. Upon their arrival, they would become man and wife. Filled with a dream of happiness with her beloved Jim, Nancy entrusted him with her entire dowry—money she had earned while working at the Whipple manor. She then went to Lancaster to make arrangements for the important trip to Portsmouth. Soon she would be a bride!

Colonel Whipple was an important man who supported the American's fight for independence. His brother William was a signer on the Declaration of Independence. Politics and war, not romance, were foremost on his mind, and he may have talked young Jim into going to Portsmouth to join the army without telling Nancy. It's possible he convinced Jim to use the dowry money to pay for a uniform, perhaps reassuring him that fighting for his country's independence was more important than wedding Nancy. The colonel and Jim secretly set out on that day, leaving Nancy behind without explanation.

Nancy soon learned of the treachery and returned to Jefferson.

On a cold day with deep snow, Nancy was determined to set out and search for the man who had betrayed her. The men at the manor tried to talk her out of going on such a dangerous journey, but she would not be dissuaded. She was familiar with the route they would be taking into Crawford Notch and felt confident they couldn't be too far ahead. It was a thirty mile trip on foot through deep snow and howling winds, but Nancy was adamant. She went off without a morsel of food. The men watched her go, believing she would return safely later in the day. But their worry grew when Nancy did not return, and at night, they too set out hoping to reach her before it was too late.

After twenty miles of hiking in the snow, Nancy came upon a smoldering fire left by Jim and the Colonel. She rekindled the fire and warmed herself as best she could. With fierce willpower, fighting hunger and fatigue, she set out again tracking the footprints of her faithless lover in the snow.

As she crossed a brook, Nancy's dress became soaked with the frigid water. She sat down next to the brook, weary and overcome.

Meanwhile the search party followed Nancy's tracks hoping to find her alive. When they reached the brook, a horrible sight awaited them. Nancy was sitting by the water, her head resting on her hand and cane, frozen to death.

Nancy was sitting by the water, her head resting on her hand, frozen to death.

Nancy was buried by the brook where her body was found. The heartbreak of this news was felt by all.

Jim, upon hearing of Nancy's death, was overcome with guilt and went mad. He died a short time later in a hospital, a broken man.

The brook, the cascades, and the hill surrounding this site in Hart's Location were given her name: the Nancy Brook Scenic Area. The spot where she was found was not far from the famous Mt. Crawford House.

The Notchland Inn replaced the site of the eighteenth century Crawford House. The property has run as an inn since the 1920s. The Crawford's tavern now functions as the Notchland's dining room. The Notchland Inn is a gracious resort, and Nancy's grave site is just a short walk down Notchland Drive and up into the woods where a large rock cairn marks the spot where she is buried. A mysterious donor once left a headstone for Nancy, and it can be seen in the Inn's parlor. Over the years guests at the Inn have reported strange occurrences. Messages have been written on mirrors when no one is around. Items are moved and then replaced.

But it is deep in the woods where they say Nancy's restless spirit still searches for her lover and for perhaps, a final answer. You can hike to the beautiful Nancy Cascades, or hike further to Nancy or

Norcross Pond. But listen closely for Nancy's cries. Her wails of sadness and shrieks of laughter are echoed in the forest and have been heard by many who visit.

THE HIKES

TO THE GRAVE OF NANCY BARTON

Nancy's cairn grave is located on Notchland Drive, just a few yards from the Notchland Inn off Rte. 302. This is a dead end road with a small trail heading off to the right from the end of the turn-around, past the inn on the right hand side. Look for a pine tree and a sign that simply states "trail." This trail leads you to Nancy's grave about twenty yards from the road area.

The Hike to Nancy Cascades

NANCY POND TRAIL

The trail leaves Rte. 302, 1 mile east of Notchland Inn. The trail follows an old road well marked with yellow painted signs. It follows an old logging road for 250 yards, diverges left and crosses a brook. It then joins a logging road on Halfway Brook, then turns right and crosses Halfway Brook, and enters Nancy Pond Scenic Area. The trail continues to a WMNF boundary which is marked by a pile of painted stones at .8 miles. Then it follows an old logging road along Nancy Brook. After a brook crossing 1.6 miles the trail diverges left. At 1.8 miles the trail goes through a series of rough landslides and re-crosses the brook, and reaches the cascades at 2.4 where the brook falls over a steep ledge and into a scenic pool.

You may choose to continue along the trail to reach Nancy Pond. At the pool, the trail turns left and climbs steeply up a series of switchbacks. The trail passes to the top of the cascades, which arc over a hundred feet high. The trail winds its way through a spruce forest to the northeast shore of Nancy Pond at 3.4 miles.

A moderate but steep hike to Nancy Cascades via Nancy Pond Trail 2.4 miles.

Time:	Allow 2 hours. To Nancy Pond via Nancy Pond Trail, 3.5 miles. Allow 3 hours. Steep and rough.
Parking:	WMNF parking fee
What to look and listen for:	Trail mostly follows along the brook. Scenic cascades and falls. Listen for Nancy's cries and laughter in the deep woods. Nancy's grave is located on a short trail through woods at end of Notchland Drive.

B18 Bomber Path - Mt Waternomee
North Woodstock, NH
2.2 miles

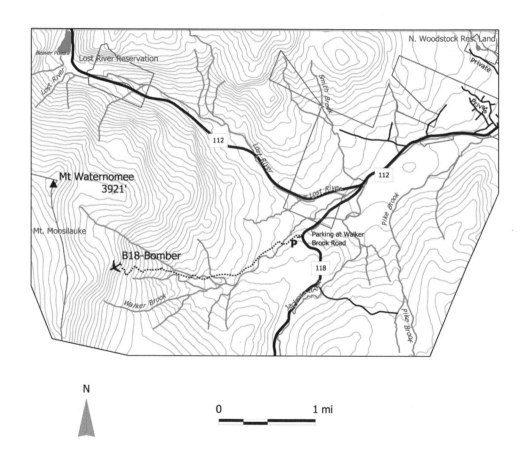

12 Mt. Waternomee's Bomber Plane—A Crash that Altered Fate

January 14, 1942, just a few weeks after the Japanese bombing of Pearl Harbor, the possibility of another foreign attack on US soil seemed imminent. On a cold, snowy night in the quiet towns of Lincoln and Woodstock, folks were going about their usual business. It was a typical Wednesday night. Men drank beer at the Lincoln Hotel bar and sank their coins into the juke box. Dr. Handy was playing a game of bridge with some friends. Lincoln High School students were up to some silly shenanigans at a mock wedding for their school fund raiser. And there was a basketball game at Donna Ross Hall in North Woodstock.

At 7:30 p.m., an alert Mrs. Huott was getting into her car when she saw it: a low flying aircraft overhead, heading straight for 4,000 foot Mt. Moosilauke. The woman gasped, and soon an explosion shook the ground like an earthquake, sending a wave of shock from Woodstock to Plymouth twenty miles away. Had the Japanese bombed the tiny village in the White Mountains? Soon after the jolting tremors, the bars emptied, the high school students fled the gym, and everyone's eyes went to the skies. Another deafening explosion followed, and Mrs. Huott drove frantically to police chief's home to report what she saw. Word traveled fast, and in the moments that followed the first explosion on that Wednesday night in 1942, the fate of seven men hung in the balance. The risks taken by the town's folk will ultimately be attributed to not only saving lives, but altering destiny.

The crash on the mountain sparked a rapid chain of events. There was no time to waste. Dr. Handy raced home to change into winter ski clothes, and then stuffed his pockets with supplies. Sherman Adams, head of a local timber company and elected town official, also saw the fire on the mountain near one of the Dartmouth Outing Club's camps. He quickly notified others by phone, including a selectman, Charles Doherty. The group drove out in the snow to Mt. Waternomee where the bomber had crashed.

Miles up the desolate wooded and trailless peak of Waternomee, seven men aboard the B-18 bomber lay in bloodied heaps in the deep snow just below the 3,900 foot summit. The twin engine bomber had left Chicopee Falls, Massachusetts, during the day on an anti-submarine patrol over the Atlantic Ocean. It was on the trip home when the trouble began.

In the blinding snow squalls and fierce wind gusts, the plane flew hundreds of miles off course. The pilots, Lt. Benvenuto and Lt. Kantner, believed at one point they were flying near Providence, Rhode Island. Further burdening the doomed journey was ice build-up and a faulty navigator. The pilots aboard the bomber were also inexperienced in handling B-18s; they were trained in flying B-24s. With the ice situation worsening, and not knowing their location, Lt. Benvenuto dropped the plane's altitude and instantly flew head on into Mt. Waternomee. In the crash, trees were leveled, some even split in two. The plane was ripped into a scattered heap of metal chunks and leaking fuel sparked a fire. A 300-pound bomb was in danger of exploding.

Below, at Sawyer Road, a hodgepodge group collected. The crew was made up of students, timber workers, Dartmouth Outing Club skiers, and members of the forest department. They began a dangerous and grueling ascent up the mountain. The snow was so deep that each of the men had to take turns breaking a path with snow shoes. They had no knowledge of what they might encounter as they bravely headed into the darkness with their dim kerosene lamps and flashlights. They climbed in snowy conditions for three hours, calling out into the night, not really expecting an answer. Suddenly, they stopped in their tracks. Staggering down the mountain just in front of them were three dark figures in blood-soaked uniforms, looking like zombies in the snowy night. They were all in a state of shock, not even knowing where they were, and badly in need of treatment. Dazed and exhausted from the ordeal, the three men did not believe that any more of their crew members could have survived after the plane's explosion. The doctor arrived to give the men first aid and apply splints to their broken bones. The search group split as one group helped the three men back to the highway while the others continued up the mountain toward the wreckage. Miraculously, they found two more of the men alive, but they were in extreme distress. One had his leg wrapped around a tree and was on the verge of freezing to death. Of the seven airmen the remaining two were believed to be dead. Sherman Adams was then notified of the situation at the base and coordinated an effort with the Red Cross. His wife was a member of the local chapter. Even more crucial in getting the men down in time was the formation of a trail through the snow and thick trees. The woodsman from Parker-Young responded and cut through the over growth to form a trail. Hours passed. The pilots were worried about the bomb that could blow the town

> *Miles up the desolate wooded and trailless peak of Waternomee, seven men aboard the B-18 bomber lay in bloodied heaps in the deep snow just below the 3,900 foot summit.*

to smithereens. Finally, after a six-hour descent of the mountain, the rescuers met ambulances at the bottom and the other two injured men were taken to the hospital.

The emotional rescue bonded the locals with the surviving airmen. Incredibly, five of the crew survived the crash, but spent a long time in the hospital recovering. The army was called to the site to detonate the bomb with dynamite. Once more, deafening explosions ripped through the town and houses shook. It was then decided by Army officials that the plane would remain forever on Mt. Waternomee. It was too risky to remove all of the pieces and fragments. After the two dead airmen were discovered, their charred bodies were removed from the site and sent home for burial.

As the men recovered from their injuries, Lt. Kantner was disappointed that he would miss an opportunity to fly home to California to see his family. He had been scheduled to take a TWA transport flight home, but because of the crash he had missed his flight. Later he learned that the TWA transport flight he missed had crashed on Table Rock Mountain in Nevada. Everyone in the crash was killed, including movie star Carole Lombard. If Kantner had not been in the crash at Waternomee, he would have certainly died on the TWA flight instead.

The crash at Waternomee became part of the lives of everyone who assisted with the rescue for years to come. Sherman Adam's quick thinking and critical direction defined him as a leader, and he later became Governor of New Hampshire. Lt. Woodrow Kantner eventually retired to Florida and became a real estate developer.

He named his marina complex "Lost River," after the name of the crash site. In 1981, he returned to the crash site, hiking to the top of Waternomee to view the wreck. He said that the crash was a part of his life, and that he is alive because of it. Kantner and Richard Chubb, who also survived, remained in touch for years.

On July 4, 1992, fifty years after the famous crash, a plaque was ceremoniously dedicated at the crash site. It is displayed on a boulder, and honors all seven men on board. An American flag also stands over the remaining scattered pieces of the plane. The site just below the summit of Waternomee today is still a graveyard to the engine parts: controls, cables, wing pieces and many shards of broken glass and metal. You can hike to the crash site and see these pieces of aircraft yourself. But don't take away any souvenirs, the plane is official property of the Federal Government.

The Hike

Bomber Path, North Woodstock

It is often called the Moosilauke Bomber; the amazing site of the 1942 crash is actually on the wooded southeast slope of Mt. Waternomee (3,921'). In a fierce January blizzard the bomber flew off-course and crashed into the side of the mountain killing two crew members.

The hike to the bomber crash site is a tough and challenging climb through thick woods. The path is not maintained or well marked and the grading is often steep and rough. Park at the gated entrance to Walker Brook Drive, on the right from Rte. 118, less than a mile southwest from the junction of Rte. 118 and Rte. 112 (or the first left after the Ravine Lodge Road). The first mile follows an old gravel logging road to its end. This section of the trail crosses over several streams that flow into Walker Brook. The trailhead is on the northwest side of the turn-around, and it is marked with a cairn. The path is marked with orange flagging, but often, the flagging falls from the tree branches. The hike will require diligence and careful tracking, as the path is not always obvious. Initially it follows Walker Brook, and then crosses over.

(No foot bridge.) After the brook crossing, the path begins a steep climb, following what might be an old logging ditch. As you make your way toward the wreckage at about 2.1 miles, you begin to notice bits and pieces of charred and twisted metal. The trail leads first to a wrecked engine, then to a plaque on a boulder with an American flag. Other parts of the fallen bomber are scattered around the area, including a section of wing, landing gear, and many unrecognizable bits of fuselage. Total distance is 2.23 miles.

Photo of author at the bomber wreckage, Mt. Waternomee.

From logging road at Walker Brook Dr. is approximately 2.3 miles of rough strenuous hiking through deep woods and unmaintained trails. Trail is not well marked.

Time:	Allow 3–4 hours.
Parking:	No fees
What to look for:	The amazing plane wreck and scattered pieces of the 1942 wreckage. Also look for the bronze memorial plaque dedicated in 1992.
For additional information:	Upper Pemigewasset
Historical Society:	www.logginginlincoln.com

Coppermine Trail - Bridal Veil Falls
Fraconia, NH

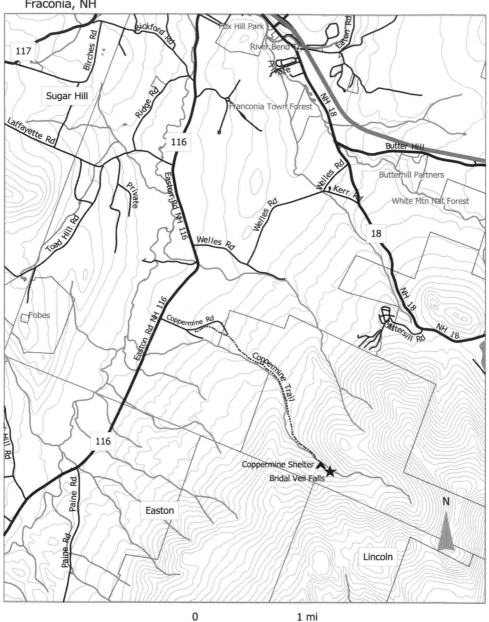

13 The Keeper of Stray Ladies

S ugar Hill is the epitome of a quaint New England town. Not much has changed in the last fifty years: Harman's still sells the sharpest cheddar, and the Sugar Hill Sampler offers up the tastiest homemade jams in Franconia Notch. Every June, Sugar Hill, along with a host of other small communities, holds a lupine festival, a week of quiet celebrations and garden sales centering on the purple wild flowers that sprinkle the fields and meadows.

Sugar Hill has its share of stories and legends. One combines love, tragedy, a mysterious plaque, and a Hollywood starlet, and connects the unlikely locations of Hollywood, California, to the quiet western hills of Franconia Notch. The story still evokes gossip and raised eyebrows. There are theories and there have been accusations of murder. Even today, many still wonder about what really happened to Arthur Farnsworth, the Keeper of Stray Ladies.

With her bold and dynamic style, feisty wit and vulnerability, Bette Davis was Hollywood's leading actress for Warner Brother's films in the 1930s and '40s. Ms. Davis was known for her fiery passion and wild temperament. Her drive and ambition were so intense, she always got her way. She was both feared and admired by those who knew her, but she always had difficulties with close relationships. When Ms. Davis wanted something, nothing would stop her.

In the summer of 1939, Ms. Davis longed for a simple and pure romance in the rocky mountains of Franconia. Having been born in Lowell, Massachusetts, she had ties to New England and frequently visited. Her career had reached a high point, and at age 31, she had already won an academy award. The debut of *The Private Lives of Elizabeth and Essex* was to debut in Littleton, New Hampshire. With the excitement of the premier, Ms. Davis took advantage of the White Mountain locale by taking a much needed vacation at Peckett's Inn, a resort in Sugar Hill. The wear and tear of a celebrity lifestyle left her ill. Surely, the country air at Peckett's, hikes on mountain trails, and the surrounding beauty of Franconia would rejuvenate her spirit and maybe spark fresh romance.

The object of Ms. Davis affections was Arthur Farnsworth, a manager at Peckett's. Farnsworth was also an aircraft engineer and airman, and it is said that Bette was instantly smitten with him, believing that he would fill her life with simple charm and uncomplicated joy.

As Peckett's manager, it was Farnsworth's duty to see to it that all the guests were accounted for at the day's end. Often, this meant heading out to hiking spots where perhaps a guest may have wandered off a trail. With this in mind, Bette herself became lost one day that summer off the Coppermine Trail. This wooded trail leads to the gushing Bridal Veil Falls that crash into deep pools over cliffs and ledges. Sure enough, as fate would have it, Farnsworth rescued Miss Davis, and the two soon fell in love. After all, how could Farnsworth resist those blue Bette Davis eyes? In December 1940, "Farny," as Bette lovingly called him, were married. The couple had begun a construction project of a summer estate

He was suddenly stricken with violent convulsions and screamed out in blood curdling shrieks as he fell to the sidewalk.

they named Butternut, located nearby Peckett's in Sugar Hill. It was to be the house of their dreams! Far from the dazzle of Hollywood, Bette was at last able to relax and live the kind of life she longed for.

Bette Davis continued her acting in Hollywood, working on a number of films. Farney, though, couldn't join her. Because of the war, he was called to work at Honeywell in Minnesota for secret projects involving aircrafts. Lonely and desperate for affection, Ms. Davis may have indulged in secret love affairs. Farney had his own extramarital relationships, one of which may have lead to the ultimate tragedy. . . .

By 1943, the marriage was on the brink of disrepair. On a warm afternoon in August of 1943, Farnsworth was walking down Hollywood Boulevard, following a lunch meeting with his lawyer. He was suddenly stricken with violent convulsions and screamed out in blood curdling shrieks as he fell to the sidewalk. Blood gushed from his nostrils and ears and a frenzied crowd gathered. A briefcase, which he had been carrying, disappeared amidst the chaos of the scene. Farnsworth was rushed to the hospital by ambulance where he lapsed into a coma. Two days later, he was dead at age thirty-three.

How could a healthy man collapse and die on the streets of Hollywood? The Hollywood Homicide Bureau opened an investigation into Farney's mysterious death. Was his secret work on aircrafts somehow related to his strange death? The medical examiner, Dr. Homer Keyes, the County Surgeon, charged that Farnsworth did not die as a result of falling on the sidewalk. Keye's report shedded some disturbing light on the mystery: he stated that Farnsworth's death was caused by a "basal skull injury," possibly as a blow to the head from a blunt instrument. Dr. Keyes noted that the blood on the fracture was congealed and blackened, consistent with a forceful blow to the head received weeks prior to his death. The doctor's findings lead to an inquest jury who called Bette Davis to testify.

Bette took the stand and assumed the role of the tragic, grieving widow. She testified to the six men on the jury that Farney had fallen at their summer home, Butternut. He was apparently running to answer the telephone when he slipped and fell down the stairs and banged his head. He had complained of headaches after the fall, she testified, but never saw a doctor. Later, Bette's personal doctor took the stand and offered his own testimony supporting Ms. Davis. Yes, he had known about Farnsworth's accident at Butternut, but had not examined him. Further muddying the story was the date of the accident at Butternut; Davis claimed the fall happened months earlier. The autopsy surgeon disputed Ms. Davis statements and declared that the fracture to Farnsworth's skull was not consistent with her account of his head injury. The medical evidence didn't add up.

Despite the contradictions in stories and evidence, the jury sided with Bette Davis and her personal friend and family doctor, Dr. Paul Moore. The inquest verdict declared that Farnsworth's death was a result of the accident at Butternut. The case was closed, the files sealed, and the original autopsy report has since been destroyed. The investigation into Farny's death came to a crashing halt, but the gossip did not.

Farnsworth was set to be buried at the beloved Butternut estate back in Franconia. But his family in Vermont disputed the burial and obtained orders to have his body exhumed and reburied at the family vault in Rutland, which was to be his final resting place. In a state of depression and nervous exhaustion accompanied by bizarre behavioral antics, Bette returned to Hollywood after the funerals to resume work. In December of 1943, while filming *Mr. Skeffington,* she was treated for an eye irritation. As the actress put drops into her eyes, she screamed out in agony and was rushed to the hospital. Someone had put acetone in her eye drops—a poisonous liquid which would have blinded her. The culprit was never found.

As the years passed, stories about Farnsworth's real killer continued. One story implicates an irate husband who caught Farney romancing his wife and struck him in the head. Other stories involve Bette in an altercation with Farnsworth at a train station where she pushed him from a platform, angry that he had been buying gifts for other women.

In Chicago, 1961, Bette reportedly met with Tennessee Williams, Frank Merlo, and a Hollywood columnist, Darwin Porter. After a few rounds of drinks, Bette was coaxed by Tennessee to reveal the story of how Farney *really* died. Bette told the group she came home early from the studio one day and discovered Farnsworth with another actress, pin-up girl Ann Sheridan. Ann fled from the bedroom while Bette confronted her cheating husband. She then grabbed a wrought iron lamp and hit him on his "two-timing skull."

After Farnsworth died, Ms. Davis's visits to New Hampshire became less frequent and she sold the Butternut estate in the 1960s. Soon after the sale, a mysterious plaque appeared in the Coppermine Brook, where years before Bette Davis was rescued by the handsome man of her dreams.

Bette Davis placed this mysterious plaque in the Coppermine Brook, Franconia.

The plaque is on a rock at the water's edge, the spot believed to be where Bette was rescued. It is hidden from the casual passerby, just as the true story of Farnsworth's death remains unknown. Bette Davis passed away in 1989 after a battle with breast cancer. She is buried at Forest Lawn in the Hollywood Hills. On her gravestone it reads, "She did it the hard way."

THE HIKE

COPPERMINE TRAIL TO BRIDAL VEIL FALLS, FRANCONIA

Hike to the beautiful falls (elevation 2,100') and see if you can find The Keeper of Stray Ladies bronze plaque.

This trail begins at Coppermine Road off Rte. 116 in Franconia. The Coppermine Road is 3.4 miles south from the junction of Rte. 116 and 18. Park at the beginning of the road, as there are signs designating where not to park. Walk up Coppermine Road for .4 miles, and watch for signs for the trailhead on the left. The trail to Bridal Veil Falls begins at the left and is marked by a sign. At 1.0 the trail joins with the Coppermine Brook and ascends steadily at moderate grades. A small bridge crosses the brook at 2.3 miles then passes the Coppermine Shelter. The trail ends at the lovely Bridal Veil Falls at 2.5 miles. This is a wonderful hike for families and even younger children.

Hike to the plaque:

Look for the plaque that Bette Davis placed in the brook approximately .25 miles from the junction of Coppermine Road and the Coppermine Trail. The plaque is fastened to a boulder in the brook. Alongside the trail at the shore line, look for a series of camp fire pits along the bank. The plaque is located near this area just about 20 yards upstream. The plaque is tricky to locate, but it is there!

Total distance from Rte. 116 is 2.5 miles. Parking at Coppermine Road. Coppermine Trail to Bridal Veil Falls

Hike estimation:	From Coppermine Rd, via Coppermine Trail: 2.5 miles
Time:	Allow 2 hours
Parking:	Park at parking area on Coppermine Rd. No additional parking beyond this point. WMNF fee area.
What to look for:	Beautiful Bridal Veil Falls at the trail's end. Also, the famous bronze plaque in the brook about .25 miles on Coppermine Trail from junction with Coppermine Rd. Plaque is located in the brook.

WHERE IS THIS PLACE?

The Coppermine Trail in Franconia is easy to find. Trail head parking is located on Coppermine Road off Rte. 116. You can hike out to the falls and take a dip in the cool water. You can also hunt for the mysterious plaque in the brook. But don't get lost, or Farney himself may come looking for you!

14 The Willey Family Tragedy and a Visit from Beyond the Grave

The expression, "give me the willies," was born from a chilling tragedy that killed nine people. The saying refers to a feeling of dread, discomfort, and foreboding. In the very heart of Crawford Notch a boulder marks the site where the Willey House once stood. There is nothing left of it. The famous flood of the Saco River in 1826 created a killer slide off the mountain behind the Willey's Inn. That mountain, Mt. Willey (94,260'), is named for the protective father and husband who perished along with his family and two hired men.

Sam Willey was a father of five children ranging in ages from three to thirteen. He was married to Polly Lovejoy from the town of Bartlett. Willey purchased a house from Ethan Crawford in the fall of 1825. With two hired men, one of them a twenty-year-old "adopted" son, David Nickerson, Sam Willey began to make improvements to the property, turning it into a popular inn. The Notch turnpike, as Rte. 302 or Crawford Pass was known then, provided an important link to Vermont and Maine. Winters in Crawford Notch were extreme and guests of the Inn were grateful for the warm accommodations Sam and his lively wife provided.

As spring approached the Willeys continued to add to the inn, but a sudden storm provoked a dangerous slide from the mountain behind them. A rushing sea of mud, vegetation, and rock had barely missed the home. Alarmed, Mrs. Willey tried to leave the house with the children, fearing for their lives. Sam Willey recognized the potential for danger. The rock slide had come about so quickly, so suddenly, and so dreadfully close to their home, he felt the need to respond to a potential crisis. He set out at once to search for a safe shelter in the event that another slide should threaten the home. He constructed a shelter out of an old cart just a short distance from the house. He also placed a massive log behind the house to shield falling rocks. As the summer months passed though, Willey's

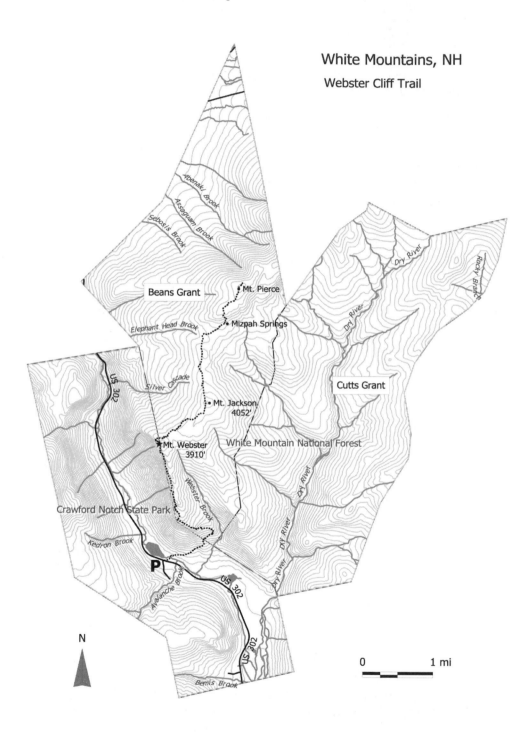

White Mountains, NH

Webster Cliff Trail

fear about a possible slide had subsided, and he calmly dismissed the concerns of guests at the inn.

The summer of 1826 was incredibly hot and dry. The drought caused the soil to blow around like powder and crops did not survive.

On the evening of August 28, thick black clouds overtook the valley like a shadow of doom. Rain fell in violent torrents. Lightning flashed in the night sky and crashes of thunder sparked fear. The Saco River rose twenty feet, carrying away sheep, pigs, and horses. The momentum of falling rock and violent rain ripped trees from their roots driving a destructive fatal path directly toward the Willey House. Three powerful slides came down from Mt. Willey, with the force of a moving sea of granite and earth.

The following day residents along the Notch turnpike began to assess the damage caused by the storm. Ethan Crawford lost fourteen sheep and all of his crops. His father, Abel, also suffered. His wife managed to survive the night while the river gushed right through their home.

A man named John Barker joined Ethan Crawford in his trek to the Willey House, which they reached late in the day. The house had escaped the ruin of the landslide. A boulder behind the house kept the home from the crushing onslaught of the killer slide. Rubble and debris surrounded the house, but it was miraculously untouched. Once inside, Barker found the rooms strangely empty, except for the family dog who barked nervously. The beds were left unmade and clothes were scattered about as if those in the house were in a rush to

According to James Willey, his brother's ghost visited him one night and explained that they were forced to leave the house because of the rising river.

flee. A bible was left opened on a table with Sam's glasses resting on the 18th Psalm. The family had quickly fled the house. By then the dog had run off, appearing some time later in Bartlett at the home of Polly's parents. The poor dog could not be calmed and before long, he too vanished from sight, never to be seen again.

The following day, Barker headed for Abel Crawford's and alerted those who were there about the abandoned house and the missing Willey family. Word quickly spread, and a team of neighbors, family, and friends began a search. On August 31 the body of David Allen, the hired help, was discovered in a heap of rubble. Right behind Allen's body Polly was uncovered with her hand outstretched to Allen's as if reaching for his assistance. Both were mangled almost beyond recognition, their faces distorted from pounding blows. Mr. Willey was found next, seventy feet away, pinned under timber and entangled in an uprooted tree. Only a few of the searchers remained in the following weeks. In September, three-year-old Sally Willey and her thirteen-year-old sister Eliza Ann, were uncovered. The last body recovered was David Nickerson. Three of the Willey children were never found. The bodies were moved to Northern Conway where the family was buried in a single mass grave. All of the children, including the ones who were never found, are included on the gray headstone.

According to James Willey, his brother's ghost visited him one night and explained that they were forced to leave the house because of the rising river. In their desperate search for safety, they were all carried away by the powerful slide. James Willey had been so haunted by the thought that if they had just stayed in the house, they would all have lived. The spirit of Sam relieved him of that anguish, insisting they had no choice but to abandon the home. There have been other sightings of the ghost of the family dog roaming up and down Rte. 302, searching for his lost family.

The Willey House was operated as a hotel until 1898, when it burned to the ground because of an unwatched candle that set a curtain on fire.

All that is left of the original Willey home site is the plaque and the mountain named for Sam Willey.

THE HIKES

SAM WILLEY TRAIL

The Sam Willey Trail is an easy hike appropriate for all levels. Park at the east side of Rte. 302 at the Willey House historical site. Leaving the road, the trail crosses a dam over the Saco River where there is a large wooden sign with trail locations. The Sam Willey Trail bears to the right, while the Pond Loop Trail bears left. The

Pond Loop Trail is a .2 mile trail offering a loop around Willey Pond with pleasant views to the mountains. It winds back and returns to the dam at the Saco River. The Sam Willey Trail follows a level path and loops around at a junction at .4 miles. Follow the trail to the left, continuing the loop where the Saco River Trail forms a junction at .5 miles. The Sam Willey Trail swings around and passes two views points of the Webster Cliffs, before returning to the loop junction at .1 mile. The complete loop is 1.0 mile.

WEBSTER CLIFF TRAIL TO MT. WEBSTER (3,910')

The Webster Cliff Trail is located on the opposite side of the Willey House Station and is 1 mile south of the Willey House site on Rte. 302 in Crawford Notch. Parking is on the right side of Rte. 302 heading east, then crossing 302 to reach the trailhead. Or, access the Webster Cliff Trail from the Saco River Trail, reached via the Sam Willey Trail, directly at the Willey historical site. The Webster Cliff Trail ascends the cliffs that form the east wall of Crawford Notch.

At .1 mile the trail crosses the Saco River (bridge). The Saco River Trail joins in at .2 miles. At .3 miles, the Saco River Trail departs The Webster cliff Trail ascends at a moderate grade up the south end of the ridge. The trail becomes steeper as it nears the cliffs. At 1.8 miles the trail opens up to gorgeous views at the first open ledge. You can choose to complete your hike here, at these marvelous ledges and views, or continue on to the summit of Mt. Webster. After reaching these open ledges, the trail becomes more gradual, and there are many view points. At 2.4 miles another ledge provides spectacular views to buildings below. Here, see for yourself how the Notch is a natural wonder; changed forever by the tragic slide of 1826.

The trail continues at a steep pitch and there are tricky ledges to scramble over. The trail reaches the ledgey summit of Webster Mt. at 3.3 miles. The views into the Notch from the cliffs on Mt. Webster are spectacular and stunning.

Mt Jackson (4,052') via
Webster Cliff Trail   ᗩᗩᗩᗩ

The Webster Cliff Trail continues north as it descends Mt Webster and continues on toward Mt Jackson. At .1 mile the Webster-Jackson Trail enters on left. The Webster Cliff Trail continues and crosses a series of wet gullies. It ascends steeply up the cone of Mt. Jackson at 4.7 miles from the junction at Rte. 302.

Willey Historic House Site Crawford Notch:
Historic House Site and museum open year round admission is free. Crawford Notch State park: (603) 374-2272

From Historic Willey Site:
Sam Willey Loop and
Pond Loop: Easy hikes reached from parking at
                              Willey House and crossing Rte. 302
                              to Pond Loop. Hike around Pond is
                              easy, less than .5 miles and will take
                              thirty minutes. Sam Willey Trail Loop
                              is 1.0 mile and will take under an
                              hour.
Webster Cliff
via Webster Cliff Trail: 3.3 miles to Webster Cliff
                              summit with amazing views.
Time: Allow 4 hours
Parking: Parking area is 1 mile south
                              of Willey Historic Site on Rte.
                              302. WMNF fees apply.
For more information: AMC (603)466-2727

Parking passes are available at AMC Pinkham Notch Visitor Center and at WMNF Ranger District Stations and any WMNF visitor center.
Pemigewasset RD in Plymouth: (603) 536-1310
Ammonoosuc RD in Bethlehem: (603) 869-2626
Forest Supervisor in Laconia: (603) 528-8722
Androscoggin RD in Gorham: (603) 466-2856
Saco RD in Conway: (603) 447-5448

AMC Pinkham Notch Visitor Center :
(603) 466-2727
WMNF Gateway Visitor center Lincoln:
(603) 745-3816

WHERE IS THIS PLACE?

There are many options to choose from when planning a day's hike from the Historical Willey House site on NH Rte. 302. For an easy hike, there's a beautiful loop along the Sam Willey Trail on the Saco River. The climb to Mt. Webster, at 3,910 ft., is a challenging hike, but the views from Webster Cliff are stunning. From this vantage point you will see for yourself how the incredible storm of 1826 forever changed the landscape. You want something tough? You can spend the better part of the day hiking to Mt. Willey, but it is a steep and treacherous climb. Yet the hard work endured upon reaching the summit will pale in comparison for what Sam Willey himself experienced 175 years ago, when his family perished in agonizing terror in the crush of an unstoppable land slide.

ACKNOWLEDGMENTS

This book is about discovery. In 2007 I attended the New Hampshire Leave No Child Inside summit and walked away with the intent to create a data base of interesting and mysterious hiking adventures for families. I began reporting these as a journalist for *The Hippo*. What happened next was *Haunted Hikes of New Hampshire*. The stories will spark yearning for adventure and mystery. The hikes will lead to possibilities of supernatural encounters! Ghosts, spirits, curses, plane wrecks, and haunted villages from years gone by are right here waiting to be rediscovered in New Hampshire. History and legend make the stories, but the people who tell them make the hikes worth while. More important, families can discover pieces of history that curiously connect them to forests, mountains, and remote landscapes. It's all about adventure and getting outside!

I would like to thank the many individuals and friends who made this possible:

Thank you Tim Trotter, Marcia LeMay, Dave Anderson, Mike "HomeBrew" Harper, Denis O'Connor, Steve O'Connor, Riley O'Connor, Curran O'Connor, Flannery O'Connor, Leah Kovitch and Lynn Kotitch and devoted hiking companion, Ruby. Patrick LaFreniere, Floyd Ramsey, Eric Pedersen, Mike Kautz, Joe Gill, Bryan Yeaton, Peter Crane, Al Rumrill, Wayne Carhart, Priscilla Weston, Bill and Judy Wolfe, Andrew Cook, Nick Finnis, Peggy Willard, Leo and Dot Turini, Ed Parsons, Peter Samualson, Friends of the Wapack, Kay Jones, Walter Caulkin, Carol Jeffreys, Lynn Clark, Pam Hess, P J Lovely, James Haddix, Steve Smith, Nick Howe, Mary Fosher, Sheila Kullgren, Morrie Gasser, Russ Dickerman, Paul Spera, Greg Kirby, Bill Malay, Peter Baker, Al Jenks, Wendy Weisiger, Lee Wilder, Marilyn Wyzga, Chris Nolan.

I would like to thank my father, Gerry O'Connor, for guiding me up my first 4,000 foot mountains in New Hampshire, North and South Hancock.I thank my mother, Elaine O'Connor, for her inspiration and belief.

Thank you Jeremy Townsend, Phil Engelhardt, and Carol McCarthy of PublishingWorks for creative direction.

ABOUT THE AUTHOR

Marianne O'Connor has worked in the Nashua School District for thirteen years. She is the mother of two daughters who often accompany her on many ghostly adventures. Marianne is a feature outdoors contributor to *The Hippo* and writes for *New Hampshire To Do Magazine* and other publications. She is an active board member of EASE (Educators Alliance Seeking Excellence) and oversees the United High School Green Team. With UHS, she is active in promoting service learning projects in conservation in Nashua.